Published by Tom Ellison
Publishing partner: Paragon Publishing, Rothersthorpe

Second Printing

ISBN 978-1-78222-808-0

Book design, layout and production management by Into Print
www.intoprint.net
+44 (0)1604 832149

Contents

Laying the foundations

The once-a-year fortnight holidays I remember as a boy, were unforgettable in so many ways. No one doubts that childhood experiences shape the person you become and for me those that surrounded a holiday, lay the foundations for what I would later seek as an adult. Looking back, this was never just a break from school, or the monotony of life, it was an experience which lasted me a whole year's worth of memories. While it could have been different for others in my family, for me, the holiday didn't start when we arrived at our destination, it began days and weeks before. I have vivid memories of preparations till this day, where it seemed both my mother and father had separate checklists. For dad it was to make sure all sheds were secure and that anything valuable or potentially dangerous would be put indoors. The day before, I can distinctly remember helping to drag most of the contents of the shed over the backdoor step, including lawnmowers, mopeds, bicycles, cans of petrol and any outdoor toys. As I have no recollection of mum having any kind of list, I assume would have simply been the contents of the cases. The night before or early in the morning, the water and electricity would be turned off at the mains, and all the sheds would be locked with at least one padlock.

My dad would pack the car the night before, leaving it on the layby outside the house. A Morris Minor has next to no boot, so the cases had to go on a roof rack which were covered in a plastic sheet to protect from the elements. These were then left outside until we re-joined them at around 3.30 in the morning. Pre M25, I think the early start was mainly to get through central London before the morning traffic took hold. As a child getting up while everyone was still asleep and tiptoeing out to a car on the layby outside, felt like we were on a secret mission. Every year was the same, we had our orders, which were to rendezvous with the car, without waking up the neighbours… although I sincerely doubt that ever happened. It was understandable that dad didn't want to advertise that the house would be empty for the next two weeks, so to reduce the risk of burglary, he would shout in a whisper half a dozen times or so, 'be quiet!'. Even now, certain parts of the journey remain in my memories, feeling so tired and trying to sleep while listening to what must have been radio 4 or world service. Try as we may, we felt we could never keep our eyes closed through London with all its sights; everything seemed to glisten and sparkle, so much traffic, so many lanes, so many lights. At around 8am or so we stopped at what seemed to be the same place every year, just south of London, for a sandwich and a cup of rotten flask tea. Then at last, the final memory that has been the same up until just a few years ago if I was honest, seeing the sea. We lived at least 3 hours away from the sea, although back in the 70's it was more like 6 hours, but this once-a-year experience was worth the wait. When we saw the mass expanse of blue shimmering water in the sun, it really did take our breath away and all we did, was gaze at it in wonder.

As I became older and had a family of my own, a group or family holiday lost much of the buzz I had experienced as a boy. Modern travel may have a lot to do with that and the fact that my wife never allows us to leave at 3.00am. This isn't because they lack excitement, quite the opposite, I work hard all year knowing that a holiday is my reward. As an adult there has to be planning, detailed planning, which means knowing exactly how we'll get to the destination and often exactly what we will do when we arrive. This in itself is no bad thing, lack of organisation on a family holiday is a recipe for wasting time, or worse. Whatever the holiday experience, I will always do my upmost to achieve maximum fulfilment, happiness and memories that last a lifetime. Although while giving my all to a family break, there is part of me that has continued to hunger for the freedom and recklessness of youth. Unfortunately, for the time being at least, the feelings leading up to and during a family holiday are not the same as those I have experienced alone. Without meaning to, some years before being married, I had made a discovery which changed everything. For many years now any 'normal' holiday excitement and experience has been relegated to second place. My journeys of discovery were about doing the unusual and experiencing what few people ever do. I will do my best to explain.

There are only a handful of people in the world who have made it to the top of Mount Everest. The few that have, one would think, are able to sit at the top even just for a few minutes and realise how privileged they are to be in that place. My discovery has quite often left me with similar feelings and perhaps because of the sand and sea, I have also dared to include 'paradise' as a description.

This book not only recounts journeys and experiences but has also caused me to uncover my motivations. It is more than tales of journeys or locations in themselves, instead, it is about why they have left such an impression. Then comes the difficult part to it all, I have rarely, if ever, been able to talk about my experiences. This being for no other reason, that it may be seen as unusual and different. From my teens I have considered myself an extrovert in terms of seeking new experiences and someone who would openly talk about them. However, as privileged an individual I have felt on my encounters, what people think has stopped me in my tracks. Therefore, I find myself with two choices, I never recall my journeys and experiences and hide them forever, or I choose to let them loose in the pages that lie ahead.

'Unchallenged'

There was a time before personal computers, before mobile phones and in our house before fitted carpets and colour TV….. this was known as 'the eighties'. I started secondary school in 1979 and before ever turning twelve this new era was upon me. There was no escaping the fact that to experience one's youth in that time was different to anything that had gone before or indeed afterwards. This decade saw innovation such as video, commonly known as VHS or BETA-MAX, MTV- a 24-hour music TV channel launched in 1981, compact discs and the first personal computers, and they weren't 'all-consuming' as much as technology is today. Although it was an exciting time of fast-moving societal change and innovation, as youngsters the majority of enjoyment was sought outdoors. In fact, when I think back to my youth, while there was time for television and music, we spent far more time seeking out other sorts of enjoyment. Until my mid-teens, bicycles and skateboards were the main form of transport and at the same time they featured in every risk-taking stunt imaginable. I remember setting up ramps to jump other kids, logs and even piles of straw on fire. We mostly stuck to footpaths, fields and farm tracks but we all rode around together in a pack inquisitively exploring new places to go and new things to do. The early years were not without mishap, there were occasions when we were chased from places we shouldn't have been and times when we were injured from just being 'out of control'. Although this kind of activity was never welcomed by our parents, there were many things we got up to that weren't actively discouraged either. One of the craziest things we got up to on bicycles when we were younger, was cycling 250 miles from Bedford to Westwood Ho in Somerset. There was no way anyone of our ages would be allowed to do what we did today, even in the age of mobile phones. I was the eldest at 16 but my friend was 15 and my 14-year-old brother came along too. Our parents agreed to meet up with us five days later but until that time we were completely on our own, with only a map and a list of campsite destinations for each night's stop-over.

By the time I was fourteen, I already had a number of 50cc mopeds and larger engine off-road motorcycles which I was able to use in the field behind our house and beyond. The hours we spent riding around the fields and farm tracks during those warm summer evenings were not only unforgettable, they made us feel like the luckiest kids… for miles around. This off-road transport took us as far as the next village, where we often met up with school friends. In many ways, the time spent on two wheeled motorised transport was no different to bicycles in as much as we still got up to the same stunts and mischief. As I recall this, I have to mention the time we raced down a concrete farm track, three-up on a 125cc trail bike. After all hanging on for dear life, we stopped so I could try a wheelie or two, but as I did, the front wheel flew off! Although a little shocking, this was typical of the thrills and spills we were used to back then. As soon as I was 16 my dad took me to a local motorcycle dealer to get my own proper road going 50cc Yamaha FS1E which was when real adventures began. Some family friends who lived in Uxbridge had children the same age as myself and my brother, and within a few months we had arranged to meet up. Although I now had road transport, this was 1984 which was still well before the age of affordable mobile phones. In fact, by this time my parents still had no landline telephone so the 70mile journey to the west of London was not only a lonely one but was without any support. Maybe things were different back then? Maybe parents trusted others more? It certainly was different and more acceptable, to let youngsters go exploring for hours on end. Although somehow, I have a feeling that when my eldest reaches sixteen, I won't be encouraging a 70-mile journey to London with or without accompanying friends and a mobile phone. That being said, my somewhat naive parents gave me the opportunity to explore and experience freedoms that many others didn't and as a result I consider myself very lucky.

A few days after my seventeenth birthday I began to take the few driving lessons I needed to pass my driving test. This was the beginning of a whole new chapter where every car I drove would be tested to its limits and new adventures would be realised. Every sole adventure and experience I'd had up to that point was training for what laid ahead behind the wheel of a motorcar. I soon discovered that a car was much like an item of clothing, it made you look good and feel good… or not. The way it was driven, its cleanliness, the music played, the generosity of the number of rides given to friends became an extension to one's personality. In essence, my popularity and ultimately the 'pulling power' for friends and girls depended on the ambiance created in the car itself, so I made sure I gave it my all. A ride in my car was an experience that took you places, and on occasion this meant actually driving somewhere. Previous to this I'd only owned a bedroom but now I had a room on wheels, somewhere to impress and entertain my friends. While some would be cautious after passing their driving test by not straying too far from home, I was the complete opposite. I passed on a Wednesday and by the weekend I had purchased a 1970's 1500cc Hillman Avenger for a hundred & forty pounds and was ready to go. I certainly started the way I meant to go on, as my very first day of driving was a spontaneous and reckless one. I drove to a local village where my friends would 'hang-out' in the local bus shelter – having little better to do. Without stopping, I slowly drove past with the windows down and shouted, "Who wants to come to London?" which was some fifty miles away. This was my first car, first time driving alone and first time I had driven in London. Even at seventeen I didn't do things by halves; I was a seize the day, maximum exhilaration, maximum experience junkie. In many respects this continues today or at least when I get the opportunity. By 10pm on Friday night I had already navigated central London, even though it was completely unfamiliar, and by the early hours a few friends and I were parked on the top of a Heathrow airport multi-storey car park, marvelling at the planes coming in to land. Back in the eighties you were able to drive into the airport carparks without a fee and get a great view of the runways unchallenged, which is certainly not the case today. When I think back to the excitement and adventure of those early driving years, it always makes me smile. Now and again when I hear a song on the radio, it transports me back in time and has even been known to cause a tear or two: Madonna, Get into the groove, Crazy for you, Tina Turner, We don't need another hero, Queen, It's a kind of magic album, Jaki Graham, Round and around, Phil Oakey, Together in electric dreams, ELO, Out of the blue album, Aha Hunting high and low album, to name but a few.

I never have been the type of person who is satisfied with just the ordinary things in life. When I think back to the experiences and discoveries of youth, I always seem to recall stories that cause others to say, "I can't believe you did that!" However, the circle of friends I spent my youth with were similar to me in many ways, always on the lookout for adventure and never shy of trying something new. If one word encapsulates those early days, while in no way attributing blame to my parents, it was 'unchallenged'. Once we were out of site, away from the house and up to our own devices, absolutely nothing was off limits. Cars and motorbikes were tested to their limits and way beyond to destruction. Working in the motor trade was great for knowing how to repair vehicles but also because it was an easy way of getting hold of a wrecker truck to pull our cars out of ditches. We each had a number of cars and as we drove around would point out where the latest off-road incident had occurred. It wasn't only cars... we were reckless with most things...

our money, our belongings and our life choices. At sixteen I remember riding back home in the evening after an event at our secondary school where we collected our exam results and were issued with the certificates to prove it. We were so crazy back then, high on life and everything it had in store for us, that we tore up the certificates as we rode along together laughing. Being there, in the moment, enjoying our definition of freedom, setting our own trends, was far more important than any future that lay ahead. There was nothing greater than 'us' and the friendships we had created, and we weren't about to allow our future education or employment define who we were, or would become. In every sense, we were totally consumed by everything around us, our cars, our music, our clothes, our girlfriends, nothing was more important.

It was commonplace to stay out till the early hours and we would often be out driving until it got light or be found asleep in a layby somewhere. If we weren't sleeping in cars, we would crash round a friend's house or on occasion camp out with friends in a farmer's field. I remember one-night camping beside a wood, where we lit a fire, and with a couple of bottles of wine, had a whale of a time. The highlight, of this particular night, was being frightened to death by something scampering around near the tent in the early hours of the morning. We couldn't decide whether it was rats, ducks or something else and this caused so much commotion that it roused the attention of occupants of a nearby house, who approached shouting and waiving a torch. An instant midnight exodus, meant the campsite was abandoned until we returned the next day, when we collected what we had left behind. The 'duck-rats' as they became known, featured heavily in future stories of midnight camping adventures and strange creatures that could be heard in the undergrowth.

Apart from cars, motorbikes and girls, there was a lack of leisure facilities in the immediate vicinity of our local village, and because of this, most evenings would be spent sitting in the bus shelter, which was the focal point for most of the village's youth. However, just outside village was a small reservoir created by a local farmer and fenced off with clearly marked 'private property' signs. Of course, this was no deterrent, so in the summer months we would occasionally visit for a dip. I never remember anyone deliberately turning up with trunks or a swimsuit and we would strip down to our underwear instead. The lack of swimsuit, was probably because at a moment's notice, we may have to throw our clothes back on and make a run for it. On occasions, depending on the company, we took everything off and enjoyed the thrill of skinny dipping. However, mixed swims were short lived as some of the boys told tales on the school bus of which girls they had seen, and the nude event remained as a topic of conversation for some time afterwards. The boys of course, couldn't give a toss that anyone knew they were nude, but the girls thought twice before going all the way in the future.

Exhilaration, fun and experimentation were the name of the game. If we had never tried something, the experience was up for grabs, and one by one, most of us had a go. Whether it was smoking, sex or drugs - such as tripping out on magic mushrooms or even hyperventilating until we fainted. The experiences were seen as rites of passage and not doing something, didn't ever seem like a choice. Personally, however, after over doing it with some homemade elderflower wine at sixteen, any future experimentation was done cautiously and in moderation. While I personally may have been a little timid, the group of teens I hung around with seemed to know no limitations and got up to all the things kids got up to, sometimes alone and on occasion in full view of everyone watching. At this point, it's better not to go into detail, except to say that twenty of us playing strip poker together was just seen as mild titillating fun. If there was any evidence required to prove that we were youth of the eighties, it was that the term 'inappropriate' was unknown to us. Apart from embarrassment, some experimentation was downright dangerous, and we rarely decided we had taken things too far. For a joke any of us would, while driving, ask the passenger to hold the steering wheel while we left the driving seat and jumped into the back of the car. Another version of this was when we at considerable speed would climb out of the driver's window, again into the back seat of the car but via the outside. Thrills and spills weren't awful accidents but badges of honour and so when my brother crashed his Suzuki AR125 on a sharp bend ending up in a ditch, he became quite a star. The whole incident was seen by two friends out walking, who rushed to his aid and congratulated him on how amazing it looked. Later that night the story was retold a number of times, of how this amazing incident took place. We once decided we would explore a derelict bungalow, as it had been uninhabited for many years. Once inside, we took turns in putting the frighteners up each other, in saying that we could hear someone coming. At one point we were all convinced we should leave and decided to get out quick; some of us were inside and others had clambered onto the roof. In the panic, a friend jumped off the roof and landed on a reinforced concrete coal bunker which collapsed as he hit it. As he clambered out it was obvious that he had been injured and was clutching his neck. It became evident as we ran home across the fields, that his injured neck turned out to be a severe puncture wound now pouring with blood. It looked so bad, that at the time we actually thought he would die, and that we would end up in a lot of trouble. Luckily, this turned out to be a story to add to the catalogue of near misses. During my youth I actually used to believe that although something was dangerous, we had a safe way of going about it. For example, we used to love lighting fires in order to explode as many aerosol cans as possible. My mum would often tell us off for blowing up a brand-new can of polish or fly spray. Sometimes they made such an explosion that the sound could be heard right through the village. I told a friend from school what we'd been up to and he decided to have a go. Although somehow, he ended up walking back to it, as the can exploded and hit him in the eye. This kind of thing never happened to us, as when we knew something was dangerous, we treated it with the respect it deserved. At the edge of the village, there was a medical facility which had large bottles of compressed air and oxygen. I was convinced that one of these would make the mother of all explosions and carried the heavy object off into the middle of a local wood. I made a fire, threw it on and cycled home as fast as I could, but unfortunately there was no distant thud to be heard. Although this was a failure, I thought perhaps this had been a little too dangerous and decided to keep the experiment to myself.

By the time of my late teens, I had begun to carry out sole adventures. Although I would travel alone on foot, bicycle or motorbike…. the journeys by car, were by far the most exciting. I absolutely loved driving alone in London and would set off late in the evening to deliberately get lost amongst the many lanes and lights. It was such a contrast to the quiet country roads and sleepy villages, and I found the whole experience mesmerising. I drove in London many times with friends, or alone enough to be able to find my way around. I could easily find all the tourist spots, like Buckingham Palace, Tower Bridge and Leicester Square, but as well as that, I could also find the back streets of China Town and Soho. I would often abandon my car in a side street and go on walkabouts to sample the atmosphere. In the busy places like Trafalgar Square or Covent Garden it was safe to be alone but if you took a wrong turn you could find yourself being approached by some unsavoury characters. Although some areas were less safe or less desirable, I loved the character and atmosphere of all of them. I would often drive around central and west London until the small hours of the morning with the window down as I reached the busy areas. There was nothing more exciting than sampling the sights and sounds of Regent Street and Piccadilly Circus at 2'oclock in the morning. I never really shared the way driving through London made me feel, it was my experience, my own enjoyment, and I loved it. Eventually, when overcome with tiredness, I would head north, find the north circular road and take the A1, A10 or M11 ...... some sixty miles north back home to bed.

My lone adventures to London during the weekend or late at night, paved the way for future pursuits. I had proved to myself that I could go it alone in the middle of London and now this made other adventures seem less of a challenge. Although I didn't realise it at the time, these early years of adventure, excitement and pushing boundaries, set the scene for what would happen next. London was to be nothing compared to my future adventures, but pre 1994, I was oblivious to what laid ahead.

'A mad few days in France'

Although I had been to this place in France several times before, I would never see it as just another visit. For me, every encounter, was a whole new adventure. What I would take, the mode of travel and even getting a pitch on the campsite itself, were never really for certain. Why would I do it any other way? A last-minute grab for essentials, had now almost become part of how I went on holiday. If I was going as a group or with the family, pre-planning and lists had their place. However, it was just me, and I had almost four days not to apply any rules and make myself smile inside by doing the things I loved. So, it was decided, the destination set, for what I had named on a word document as 'a mad few days in France'. There was no plan, just a list of flight and train times, taxi numbers and possible campsites. Although I knew where was going …. the word document and lists I'd left around the house, stated the destination as Biarritz. The definition of a holiday is different for everyone; it may be the beach, scenery, food, the language or just a change from normality. For me it's a lot of things, I love swimming and especially snorkelling- in the sea, camping, the beach, driving in a foreign country, but for some years now I've wanted more. There's no doubt that part of me is trying to rekindle the excitement and adventure I felt when I was younger, but that's not the whole reason.

The day of the trip was upon me before I knew it. Although this was the way I did things, some inner nerves made me wish I had applied a little more rational thinking. I hate flying, I have no tent, I don't know if my bag will fit everything in, what if the site I want to go to is full? There's just over an hour before my father-in-law is giving me a lift to the airport and I'm just back from work. The immediate priority was to gather together the few items I was taking….. goggles, shorts, four tee shirts, sandals, wallet, three pairs of pants and my print-out of train and flight ties. For some reason, the next thing I had to do was go for a run. This bit, even for myself, is hard to explain apart from it has something to do with me and flying. I hadn't flown for some years and was feeling a bit stressed about the whole idea of it. Surely, I'm not the only one who feels like it's just not normal being stuck in a tube at 35,000 feet! When it came down to it, the run made no sense at all, but it made me feel like I was fit and could breathe, and in some way if I could do that I could probably cope with the physical exertion of flying. I didn't go too far, just a couple of miles before heading home, a quick shower, bag packed with essentials, bank cards, 300 euros, passport, no tent, I was ready. As I was dropping my wife in it looking after a one-year-old for a few days, apologetically I left the house and promised not to tell her dad where I was going. She thought that it just wasn't the done thing to go away without your wife on holiday. Although we had agreed this was ok, explaining this to her family could be avoided and we decided was best.

On first impressions, one could be excused for thinking that my father-in-law is abrupt and perhaps even rude, however this couldn't be further from the truth. Whilst he certainly isn't slow to say what he thinks, he wouldn't think twice before dropping everything to help anyone in need. He hammered on the door and ran back to the car to wait. A quick kiss goodbye and that was it, I'd left 'normality' and I was off for a 'mad few days in France'. It seemed odd leaving the house in shorts, tee shirt and sandals, as it really wasn't the warmest of days, and a coat may have not have been a bad idea. As I got in the car I was greeted by, "Are you ready?" which while I politely answered…. was talked over with,

"Have you got everything?" I think he meant that I may have forgotten something important, like my wallet or passport? My reply to his question was a stupid one…….. without thinking.

"No actually, I haven't got my tent!" What a plonker, why did I say that now he'd wonder where I was going and what I needed a tent for. While I was thinking how stupid I'd been he replied,

"Do you need to get it?" Now I really wish I hadn't replied to the 'have you got everything' question. I'd never really thought I was that high on his estimations regarding intellect, so my reply just confirmed his belief in me.

"Actually, I don't need a tent … now, I'm picking one up from my brother's house". There I go again I'd said something else which didn't make sense. Why did I need a tent? 'Ask me … go on?' I thought to myself.

"Ok, are you ready to go?" was his stern reply. Either, he had his mind on other things, or he'd decided, that any more questions on the tent thing would result in further ramblings.

"Yes, I have everything, I've left nothing behind". I felt I now had to say this as clearly as I could, without any ambiguity. With that we were off at surprising speed, which undoubtedly would have killed any small child in the way, as we lived on a fairly busy estate. In fact, it was so fast that I thought I may have annoyed him in some way, or perhaps I was putting him out as he had other things he needed to be doing.

"Are you ok giving me a lift? Are you busy?" I threw in at an appropriate moment. This had to be away from a bend in the road or junction, as at the speed we were travelling I didn't want to cause any distraction or be the cause of any unwanted deviation.

"Yep, were you busy at work today?" He hadn't really listened, as he was applying full concentration to driving, and maybe wouldn't have detected that I was just saying something to check he was ok. I didn't want to answer the question about work, my adventure was the focus now, nevertheless I had to answer. We made some small talk for the first few miles until we approached a roundabout where any conversation was interrupted.

One of my biggest faults, is being critical about others driving abilities which in most cases would be unfair. However, it is my opinion that his driving was not only erratic, but he paid no heed to any rules of the road. In a previous life, some eighteen years ago, I had been a driving instructor and although I would like to revert to my youth in a driving sense and just go with the flow, I find it hard to not be a stickler for the correct way of driving. However, the way he negotiated roundabouts was worse than just going with the flow, it was dangerous and because of this I had made it clear to my wife that he would never be allowed to drive with any of our future offspring as passengers. We needed to turn left or at least go straight ahead for the airport but as expected he is in the right-hand lane with another vehicle already in the left lane alongside. What should I do, close my eyes and hope for the best? Which to avoid being rude or in any way critical is the option I usually favour, or do I give a helping hand, if only for the sake of the driver to our immediate left. I open my mouth and on auto pilot realising he has seconds to amend his ways, put my foot right in it.

"It's the left lane to go straight ahead"

"What!" was his reply.

"Are you not going to the airport?"

"Yes, the City airport."

At that, mayhem seemed to be all around. Already on the roundabout, now with a car behind, the brakes went on. At the same time, he muttered some noises that resembled short versions of swear words that couldn't be heard for the car horn behind and then he actually tried to turn left instead of continuing around the roundabout and reassessing the situation. I knew quite clearly...... that's what I would have done, but he wasn't me. He would never admit it, driving wasn't second nature, it was stressful and so an unplanned change in direction didn't help matters. At this point, in his defence, it has to be said that this life skill is lacking all over Ireland to the point of wrong lane, wrong signal, and especially wrong lane on a roundabout, is a common occurrence. Whilst chatting to a local church minister, addressing the fact that very few people seemed to know how to drive on a three-lane motorway. I described the situation of people driving in the middle lane whilst a handful then use the left lane for overtaking the folk that should be on the left. His reply really spoke volumes about the lack of knowledge and skill. "Yeah, it seems to be a different etiquette in England on the roads". At the time, the only reply I knew was, "actually it's not etiquette, it's the law." We did turn left, and to my amazement, we managed this without colliding with anything. Whilst we were now on the correct route, he now knew we were destined to be a further five miles away than originally intended, and this piled on the stress.

"Are you going to get there on time? What time is your flight?" He must have thought that I was so laid back. I never get to an airport on time, as I have seemed to have mastered a kind of 'last minute, make it through the gates' approach that would worry some people to insanity, but me, I thrived on such things.

"Yeah, I'll be fine, don't worry" I'm sure was ignored.

We made it to the airport in one piece, which was a bonus and I asked him to just drop me off, just anywhere. This was not the way things were done and he didn't like it at all, but after some toing and froing, he dropped me off in the middle of the road on a zebra crossing. I got out and said a quick goodbye, that got no answer at all. As I walked to the airport, I laughed out loud as I knew he was either thinking or saying that I was an idiot, but mainly because I had now started my adventure. Apart from a brief stopover at my brother's house, it was just me and my favourite thing in life, my holiday.

In my usual style, I ran up to the gate, collected my boarding pass and was told to hurry through to the gate as it was just about to close. As I hate flying, at this stage, I'm on 'auto pilot', to pardon the pun and have my passport and 'airwaves' chewing gum at the ready. I don't mind airports at all and in fact I quite enjoy the airport itself, if it wasn't for the fact that it's followed by a flight. However, with the excitement that I'm heading for warmer climates, I stand in the queue for the aeroplane with a smile on my face. Out in the open, the point of no return, I head for the front, straight up the stairs and spot the seat I want. Bag up, chewing gum out and I'm ready. Bizarre as It seems, this is how I fly. I pop in three or four pieces of gum, inhale the eucalyptus vapour and shut my eyes, this way I smell no jet fuel. This process is then repeated every ten minutes or so until touchdown, when I must discreetly dispose of a large ball of gum.

Some 45 mins later, the wheels of the plane smoothly touch down on the runway at Luton. Instinctively, everyone stands up and scrambles for their overhead luggage as if their life depends on it. A nearby passenger asks politely if I could pass his bag, which was above me and not him in the overhead locker. I reached up, brought it down and bounced it off the top of a seat headrest towards him. Outer doors open and I was away, down the steps, into the building and to my awaiting brother who lived some 20 miles or so from the airport. As I entered 'arrivals' he wasn't waiting for me, so as I was starving, went to get a sandwich. My hand went in my pocket for my wallet and …. oh flip, now what, I muttered to myself, now what am I going to do? My wallet wasn't there. I began to retrace in my mind what I'd done, and then decided that I knew exactly where it was. I had it on the plane... and now I didn't. I bet it had fallen out as I helped the guy with his bag. I knew I couldn't go back to the plane, but I could go to the customer service desk and explain what had happened. However, the conversation with the receptionist, at the desk, didn't go the way I had intended. I explained that the only place I could have lost it was on the plane and would she be kind enough to check if it had been dropped on the floor. Without picking up a radio or phone, to see if someone could check, her answer was,

"The plane would have been checked as you got off and anything found will have been taken to the lost property desk. By now the plane is locked up, so I'm afraid that's all you can do". She had really pulled out all the stops and gone the extra mile to help me. I was furious.

Sometimes in life you are totally at the mercy of the person who is delivering their version of customer service, so all I could do, was head for the lost property desk. There was only one person there, so this was my one and only chance. There was no coming back to try someone else. I wanted it to be me who had picked up the radio and enquired about my wallet, I would have known who to talk to and what to say, because this was a fixable problem. But it wasn't me, I was at her mercy. While she was talking, my thoughts were racing ahead…. 'Is this trip still on? Can I go to France without it?' She was chatting to someone, probably a mate out the back drinking tea for all I knew. There was a pause for around a minute, which of course wasn't long enough to actually check anything. An inaudible reply came back, and she repeated her colleagues' original statement, surprisingly almost word for word, which I didn't believe for a second.

"The aircraft is locked up for the night".

I explained that I was flying out again in the

morning and agreed to come back to collect the wallet. Even though this was a customer service disaster, I was kind of reassured by the logic that *the wallet* was on the locked plane and that I would simply collect it in the morning.

Now I gave my previous thought full concentration – was it on or off? I ran through a simultaneous mental and physical checklist:
- zip up top with big fluffy hood, which doubled up as a pillow
- chewing gum in pockets
- passport
- 300 euros
- a handful of clothes

Barring no other costs, I didn't need a wallet, I'd convinced myself. Tired and hungry after the stress of flying, I phoned my brother to pick me up.

I was picked up on the side of the road, as I had started walking, and the twenty-five-mile trip to his house was an uneventful one. There were only two reasons for the visit, there was no direct flight to my destination, and I'd had a tent delivered to his house. The reason for the tent was twofold; it was an inflatable one that because there were no sharp poles could be taken as hand luggage. Reason two, as hand luggage, I could quickly leave the airport, grab a taxi and make it to the railway station to catch the train I needed. The bonus was, to put it in the hold was roughly the same cost of buying the tent. This was what you call a no-brainer apart from one shocking thing, the bag it came in was enormous! I had never seen a bag as large go through as hand luggage…. this would not be straight forward at all.

After the flight, the wallet incident and the drive, all I wanted to do was eat and then sleep. I tried not to make a big deal out of it, but I had to ask if I could eat something rather than be offered some food. When it came to the sleeping arrangements he just said, "I don't know." To be fair, I'd asked to be picked up from the airport and then expected room service on arrival. I decided to take the least obstructive option, got myself some cereal and slept on the living room floor.

I decided to wait till the morning to ask if I could borrow money for the train back to the airport. He cautiously leant me thirty pounds, in the way a person would as if they thought they would never see it again. We set off early in the morning and after a short drive, arrived at the station which left me just over an hour to get to the airport. With a feeling of excitement, I waved as he left. That was it, I was alone, and my adventure was back on.

So many people I know, would find having no train planned to get to the airport… a real cause for worry, but I could never understand that kind of logic. As I queued for a ticket, I was weighed down by an awkward sized bag with a wide strap to spread the load over my shoulder. It was quite possible that the tent would never make it to France. The possibility of nowhere to sleep, not knowing if I'll get to the airport on time, and no wallet…. this was the real way to enjoy a holiday. Half a sleep, I sat on the train soaking up the atmosphere and the scenery. Although my tiredness wouldn't let it show, a smile was beginning to creep across my face. By the time I arrived at the airport I felt like I was smiling visibly. Whatever happened… I was going to France. With this in mind, I didn't really care what happened at the lost property office. However, I was somewhat perplexed when I was told that there was no wallet on the plane. It was decided, this was a cash only trip with no back-up. As I left for the check-in desk the only slight concern was that someone could be spending my hard-earned money as I had no time to phone the banks to stop the cards. There was nothing I could do, with the check-in desk in my sights, it dawned on me that the girl on the desk could stop me or make me pay for the bag if spotted. I kept it tucked behind me awkwardly, then as I was called forward, dropped it to the floor out of sight. With a sense of relief and not knowing if it would even fit in the overhead lockers on-board, I headed for security. I threw all my possessions on the conveyer belt and even before I had walked through myself, the bag was pulled to one side.

"What's in here?" I was asked as caught up with it. The man told me a long tube could be seen on the screen and he asked me what this was. "It's a pump", I said, "It's an inflatable tent." As the bag was opened and the bright yellow pump pulled out, I felt slightly embarrassed. Who brings a tent on an aeroplane? I thought to myself. Red faced, I zipped it up and headed for the boarding gate. To my amazement and subsequent relief, the bag slid effortlessly into the overhead locker, even if it was a little cumbersome to manoeuvre. The flight to my destination was uneventful. In fact, a flight is something I quickly forget. I deliberately don't want to think about it, talk about it or remember it. The excitement of getting to my destination is greater than the emotion experienced while flying. There is little else to say except I mentally do everything to remove myself from the reality of being thirty-five thousand feet above the earth and spend most of the time in conversation with my maker. When I was younger it was about the travel, the destination and everything leading up to it. It is certainly still about the whole adventure including the travel but if there's a flight involved, part of me only allows the holiday to begin as I exit the plane.

A courteous, 'thank you very much' as I exit the plane, out into natural light and.....heat! A big sigh....and ......France heat. As I walked back into the building with my ginormous piece of hand luggage, for a few minutes I relax. A short walk through the air-conditioned luggage area and carousel, then properly outside to a sign announcing a very welcoming temperature of 36c.

I had to get a taxi to the town centre railway station to catch a train. I'd intended to purchase my ticket online but for some reason there was an 'unavailable' message on the SNCF website that I didn't understand. I got the attention of the taxi driver at the front of the que.

"La gare, sil vous plait?", I said. He muttered something in French, looked at me as if waiting for an answer, then said, "Oui". Although our brief conversation made little sense, I assumed he knew where I wanted to go, so I jumped in, and was off. On arrival, I paid the driver the overpriced fee, and headed for the ticket office. There was a large clock in the ticket hall, which showed that I had just ten minutes before departure, with a significant que in front of me, it would be a close call. With three minutes to go, I got to the desk.

"Une billet pour lesspare, sil vous plait". The lady at the desk didn't speak any English and I didn't understand her reply. I shrugged my shoulders and gave a 'I don't understand' look. She left the desk and returned with an English-speaking colleague.

Apparently, the line was undergoing some repairs and all the trains to Lesspare, were now leaving from another station across town. I asked for the name of it to be written down and headed outside, I tried run to the taxi rank but couldn't, due to the weight of the inflatable tent. Annoyingly, the whole point of the tent, was so I could quickly escape the airport and catch the train, all hope of which was gone. I jumped in the next available taxi, sat back and hoped for the best. Anyone watching me arrive at station number two would have certainly laughed, as I was now running with the bag walloping my back. I pushed the door open into the station stopping to look around and take in my new surroundings. There was no line passing through, instead a set of buffers at the end of a single track that terminated at the almost deserted station. There was a lady at the ticket kiosk with two people in the que, who must have walked in just a few minutes before me. There was a train in the station, but it looked empty and not about to go anywhere in a hurry. After what seemed like ages, as the pace had slowed somewhat, I reached the ticket desk. To my dismay, I found that not only had I just missed the train but the next one was due to leave in almost three hours! I spent the time fulfilling my basic human needs...... toilet, water and food in a shop just a short walk from the station.

When the time came to get on board there was a surprising amount of people, around seventy or so and we were let onto the train about ten minutes before it left. In hindsight I wish I had not rushed to get on the train so early as it was an old train with no air conditioning. I felt like a had just crawled into a hot tin can and everything inside was slowly cooking. All the windows had been opened by its new passengers and almost everyone had fashioned a makeshift homemade fan to move the air across their body. Although I was baking in what must have been at least 40c in the train, I felt lucky as I drank from a large bottle of water, which few people had.

A short announcement came over a crackly on-board speaker and the train shunted backwards away from the station. Simultaneously, acknowledging the desperation for any movement of cooler air to flow through the carriage, a cheer erupted. Around forty minutes later, the train pulled in to Lesparre, where I ended my journey. I knew this station had a bus link but there was no bus. The few people who had disembarked, seemed to disappear like ants disturbed from under an upturned stone.

Just as I was contemplating how to travel the next 21km, a taxi drove up to the station, as no seemed to be waiting…. she had a guaranteed fare. I explained my destination and jumped in. This was the home run, the finish line, what lay ahead was my secret place. Although I'd had to tell stories of my stay in a campsite near Biarritz, I've never actually been there. The real destination was Centre Helio Marin – Montalivet, which was the first and at one point, largest, naturist resort in the world, and this was the story of the travel for my fourth visit.

My first time

Being a neighbouring country, France was always the obvious choice for a quick foreign holiday. I had only been a couple of times before, the first being a day-trip during the last year of primary school in 1979, to Boulogne. Then in 1991, myself, my brother and a friend booked a campsite, packed my mk3 Ford Escort to the roof and headed for St Jean De monts in the Vendee region, which was only the third time away with a group of friends, without parents. After venturing outside the UK, I'd discovered there was exciting potential for something new and unexpected around every corner, and decided I wanted more.

I hadn't particularly planned a holiday to France, but because of my new interest in the country, I had purchased a French camping and caravan guide ready for any future trip. It was sometime around spring of 1994, that I spotted an advert in the back inside cover, which caught my attention so much, that over the next few months I began to dwell on it more and more. I can't remember it word for word, but it was an advert for a naturist campsite in France – 'Naturissimo - Centre Helio Marin' (CHM), in Montalivet. There was only one photo, of an outdoor swimming pool featuring a group of people, obviously naked. This was well before anything like the internet, so I had little opportunity to carry out any research of the campsite. I did buy a couple of ordinance survey maps of the area which showed me where it was situated and contained transport links such as roads, railway lines and stations. The advert could have been for a small insignificant site for 50 residents or so, however sheer luck meant I had actually stumbled upon the largest naturist campsite in the world. Again, by chance, the only reason I'd discovered this fact, was from an old 1981 Guinness Book of Records I came across in a local library. Because of the photo in the advert, I'd become somewhat obsessed with naturism and what it could offer, which was obviously lots of nudity. So, I had instinctively turned to 'N' for naturism where to my surprise, I found the name of the campsite where the description read, Centre Helio Marin, Montalivet, the largest naturist campsite in the world. This discovery was made some months before going, but on learning this had significantly increased the reason to go. In fact, by 1994, unbeknown to me, this site no longer held the record for being the largest in the world but was the second busiest in terms of numbers. The thought of being there used to make my heart beat harder in my chest, I would imagine in my mind what I would see and what it would feel like to be there. I wasn't left with a choice, I had to go, and the first time I went, I wanted to go alone.

I can't remember phoning the site to book a pitch, but I do remember borrowing a small tent and a sleeping bag from a female work colleague. I had also borrowed a big bag with two handles and a strap for over the shoulders which would later break under the weight of its contents. Early September, and quite late in the holiday season, I packed the bag and got a lift from my brother down to London to catch a train which departed at 22.30. It was a warm night, and the train was packed with young people. It must have close to midnight when the train arrived at Newhaven ferry port. All I remember of the ferry, was a rush by everyone to find a good spot for their sleeping bags for the overnight crossing. I went with the crowd and did the same but remember being woken in the middle of the night to what sounded like a propeller coming out of the water followed by a shudder as the boat found its level in the sea again. While semi-conscious this seemed like a bizarre midnight dream but by the next morning had the impression that some parts of the crossing had been quite rough. We arrived in Dieppe at around 4am as first light ushered in a new day. From memory we disembarked right next to a railway line with a train in waiting. After our passports had been checked we were herded onto the new mode of transport and continued our journey. The next two hours or so was a fight to close my eyes and get some sleep, but it never happened. At 6am we arrived at Gare de Nord in Paris and although it was back in 1994, I remember it like it was yesterday. I was on my own, early in the morning in the middle of Paris and had a sick feeling in my stomach due to lack of sleep. Although I'd been apprehensive about this part of the journey, I took one step at a time, studied the line maps and kept a calm head. I found the London underground daunting at the best of times, but this was far worse, it was the Paris Metro. Although I didn't speak the language and the money wasn't what I was used to, I was impressed by how I well I managed. After winning the battle with the Metro, I arrived at the terminal where I was to catch the TGV train to Bordeaux. To my knowledge in 1994, this would have been the fastest train in Europe, if not the world. I had almost a two hour wait for its departure, again with no sleep but it was worth it. My own pre-booked numbered seat was spacious and although I just couldn't sleep with excitement I could certainly relax and close my eyes. The TGV was a fast train, I knew it, but this was close to the speed of air travel, at least I'd imagined it was, as I hadn't flown yet. At around 2pm the train pulled into Bordeaux station; still feeling tired I was now hungry too, so I went to a small station café and attempted to order a coffee. To my horror, I was given a thimble sized cup, with a shot of strong black coffee. I did need something to wake me up, but I didn't need the crippling pain of indigestion. I found another shop and bought a sandwich, some water and some pink stomach medicine which whatever it was, did the job. My next train from Bordeaux followed the local train line north until it was as close to Montalivet as the line would go. It came to a stop at Lesparre and I got off with my bag, which to this day, can still remember it's weight. I hadn't planned the journey from the station at all, but when a bus was already sitting outside the station, I was very pleased.

"Une billet pour Montilavet les bains, sil vous plait", she didn't understand a word of what I'd said but her reply saved me from attempting it again.

"Centre Helio Marin?"

Now I didn't understand what she was saying, but the next thing I did recognise.

"Naturiste?"

"Oui", I said….. and handed over some money. Like a tourist, I let her count out the correct amount and I sat down. I was between being excited and in agony during the journey and alternated between pink medicine and water which held off the abdominal pain. The coach stopped briefly at Montilavet Vendays town and then kept going towards the coast. I had studied the next part of the journey in detail on the ordinance survey map, so when we arrived at a crossroads with 'la avenue de l'europe', I knew exactly where I was. The bus turned left and travelled another kilometre along the road before coming to a stop outside of the resort entrance.

"Bloody hell!", I said out loud to myself," I'm here."

I went to the desk and showed my passport, which was an easy way of saying who I was, as I didn't speak enough French to get me a coffee let alone book myself into a campsite. Let's be honest, the first time I went, I was there as a hot-blooded male who just couldn't wait to see all the naked females inside the camp and on the beach. My motives for my first trip were not to try naturism as I didn't have a clue what that was, instead it was to enjoy the view as much as possible. Because of where I was, I had kind of expected them to ask what I was doing there, in fact I found quite the opposite. There was no interrogation, just nice friendly staff who spoke English far better than I would ever be able to speak French. I handed over some passport sized photographs and in return was given a map of how to find my pitch in 'arjonics', one of the areas of the site. It's strange to think of it now, but while I was waiting, I can remember straining to look through the windows of the reception area towards the campsite, trying to get my first glimpses of the naked clientele. After a few minutes I was given a pass, which I later attached to a string and put round my neck. I grabbed my bag and I walked off through the French heat, following the map to my pitch. Along the way I'd spotted the odd naked person but now ignored the nudity, while I had my bag and was fully clothed, I felt like I was still an outsider.

I found my pitch and nervously looked around again to see if there were any naked folk nearby. After pouring out the contents of my bag onto the forest floor, I began to assemble the tent for first time, as there had been no practice at home. As it began to take shape, my 'naked person radar' noticed people who were just casually walking past. I couldn't wait any longer, even though the tent wasn't finished, I wanted to get naked! It felt so good as everything came off, but also a little strange. I made the tent secure with my naked arse on show and then threw the bag inside. Camping didn't interest me at all, I had to explore, and having not been naked outside since skinny dipping as a teen, this was going to feel very unusual indeed. While a few minutes before I'd been in agony with my stomach, the pain was completely replaced with a cross between apprehension and pure excitement. I began to walk away from the tent on the campsite path, barefoot......as it just seemed like the natural thing to do. However, as I set off overcome by a sense of liberating freedom, my feet had at the same time been jagged by stones causing me to hobble to a halt. So, with a silly walk, trying to avoid further pain, I returned for the protection of my sandals.

I didn't know anything about the campsite, but I did know it was next to the beach, so like a child who hadn't seen the sea all year, that's where I was heading. Along the way I encountered an elderly couple who spoke no English at all and as I'd forgotten the french word for 'beach' was left with no idea where I was going. As one path led to another, eventually the canopy of pine trees thinned, and the gravel tracks became wider. A long tarmac wide road came into view that very clearly led towards beach. A beach-style clubhouse was set back to the left and before it was a large cycle park with what looked like well over a hundred bicycles. A picket fence now clearly marked the way ahead as I continued with mounting excitement and anticipation, towards a beach observation tower and the beckoning horizon.

Not only was this my first time naked in front of strangers but it was my first-time setting foot on a naturist beach. I didn't know it at the time, but this beach encounter would change everything. As the beach came into view, my lifelong instinct would have been to see the expanse of water and then the sand, but not today. "Flip in heck look at that", I muttered to myself out loud, as I stood for a while to take in the amazing view before me. The sea and the sand were both beautiful, which up until that time was probably the most picturesque beach I had ever seen. However, this was only the canvas for the painting of nudity that was spread upon it. Far into the hazy distance, each way up and down the beach, were hundreds and hundreds of people. This was something I had never seen before, or even knew existed, but it did exist, and I was there. It was one of those moments in life where everything seemed to go into slow motion, and I felt a 'thud-thud' in my chest as I walked towards the naked bodies. I had no preconceived ideas of what this type of nudity or a naturist beach would be like, and inquisitively set off to investigate.

As I walked down onto the beach, without realising it, I became one of them and instantly blended in. I found an appropriate gap between the bodies and laid out my towel on the golden sand, then sat down nervously, as if all eyes were upon me. At first, there was nothing else I could do apart from look around and take it all in. Even in those first few minutes, I began to get a sense that this was not what I'd expected. There was nothing weird about it and no awkwardness at all, it was like any other beach apart from, everyone was naked. It was filled with a surprising mixture of people, from babies through to the elderly and reassuringly there were enough single people to not make me feel like I stood out. Although this was my first time and I was as nervous as hell, after a short time, these feelings soon vanished. No one was looking at me, I was as nude as the person next to me. There was no covering up, no embarrassment, no shame, instead what appeared to be a freedom to just be nude. I got up, had a look around to get my bearings, then set off on a naked beach walk, and as I did, became aware of a totally new sensation, the sea breeze through my pubic hair. The beach was made up of sun bathers at the rear, near the dunes around ten rows deep. This mainly consisted of people lying out on towels as couples or family groups with occasional children dotted between, constructing things out of sand. Then there was what seemed to be a constant stream of people walking up and down the length of the beach, or to and from the sea. There were swimmers, surfers, people playing rackets sports and even a beach volleyball court which made me actually laugh as I walked past, as it reminded me of a scene from a 'carry-on' film. In terms of overall numbers, it was difficult to assess but it seemed as if it was more like thousands than hundreds. The initial nervousness had subsided, but I was still really excited by the new sensations and extraordinary experience I was having, as I walked along with my private parts sampling the sea air. By now I had a constant smile and an inner feeling of contentment, I felt so privileged to be there. I kept thinking to myself, if my friends back home could see me now. Just a few hours ago I was sitting on a train and yet here I was, having the most surreal experience.

I remember to this day the first time I walked into the sea naked. Although there was a wide expanse of beach, there were only two lifeguard points, each one marked by flags denoting the safe bathing space. This meant that each swimming area was busy with smiling, screaming, laughing people as naked as the day they were born. As I walked forward and felt the unusual feeling of cool sea water splash on my manhood, I was very conscious of being part of a naked crowd. I couldn't stop myself from laughing as I jumped the waves and noticed the bouncing breasts of ladies who were doing the same. During my first trip, this was my first recollection of really noticing female bodies, as of course this kind of thing up until that time was out of sight and of course, off-limits. As a young man in the close vicinity of mostly young attractive females, having a good look was inevitable and of course this was the reason I was there. However, my reaction wasn't what I'd expected. Instead of sex fuelled voyeurism, because of where I was, I found myself gazing as I would if in a crowded art gallery. This wasn't a one-to-one intimate moment, it was a public beach where the atmosphere was completely, not what I had expected. So instead, I just stood and soaked up the sights, the sounds and the feeling of it all, and my intention to gorp turned into mere observation of different female characteristics and beauty never seen before. In those first few hours I had a mixture of curiosity and eventually a simple acceptance that this was what naturism was all about. Although there were some things I'd never seen before, it didn't matter, I found there was a freedom about it that made it acceptable. I came to realise very soon after being on the beach that nudity wasn't rude or shocking, just somewhat unusual for the novice. While in the sea for the first time, I turned back towards the beach as a family of four walked past me and into the sea. I couldn't help comparing this in my mind to a normal beach and remember laughing to myself at how absurdly different this place was to normal society. The beach that day was 'a first' for a lot of things to do with the naked body. If I was honest with myself, I expected it to be an erotic experience, as nudity with the opposite sex usually would have meant that, however in this setting it couldn't have been further from it, it really couldn't. There certainly were many beautiful ladies but there were also flat chested women and old ladies with breasts almost touching their belly buttons. On the same note there were average looking men with various sizes of gut, very athletic looking men and men with penises the size of a donkey. The 'body beautiful' with all its imperfections was on display up and down the beach, men, women and youngsters.

My first time on the beach would have been just a few hours, as I had arrived late in the afternoon, but by now had been on the beach long enough to have been aware of the tide. I was conscious that it was gradually coming in and the crowded beach was being squeezed back towards the banks of the dunes. By early evening, it was becoming more obvious that there was little space left. People were apologising as they moved tighter together, as the occasional wave took out a row of towels in its reach. The naturism I had experienced up till that moment was encapsulated in my mind as unfettered innocence however there was something I'd not bargained for. As obvious as it sounds, when you start to get up close and personal to other naked people, without meaning to, more intimate parts of the body become hard to avoid. As I became more and more conscious of the closeness of bodies I remember trying to not to obviously look, even though a few hours before it was the only reason for being there. While I was making this unnecessary effort, I found that those around weren't playing their part at all, so avoiding an accidental eyeful was impossible. There was no one being deliberately explicit, but the fact was, with backsides in the air, it was occasionally in that ballpark. People were still carrying on with beach life and all its activities whilst at the same time, trying to keep themselves to themselves. Although this was now becoming less and less possible, as I discovered myself, my lack of towel space meant I could only sit and not lay down. A lady behind me apologetically stuck her foot in my back, as I turned to get an unexpected personal view of her. The situation carried on for as long as I could bare the stupidity of the lack of space, and eventually being slightly embarrassed, I made my exit.

There are always certain memories you take home with you after a holiday that last well into the autumn and winter months, however these memories would last many years. This was all part of me getting used to naturism on a close and more intimate level. No one cared who was watching or what could be seen, why would they, everyone was naked. I began to accept this as 'normal' after a few days, although at the time I was a little fazed by the whole ordeal. When you are part of a crowd of people in the same state of undress, you just act and do the same, when in Rome as the saying goes. The first day on the beach was a crash course in French naturism, and that first day gave me a lot to think about. I felt like I had been let into some secret taboo gathering where what you saw could never be talked about. Of course, the reality was, it was just naturism, nothing more. Apart from the thoughts and visions of the beach, it dawned on me that I was tired, sunburnt, and starving hungry so I headed to the campsite to check out the amenities.

In the very centre of the campsite, there was a rectangular area with grass and seating in the middle. This area was bordered by a number of shops and restaurants which included a small supermarket. In the centre of the grass area there was a mini take away style food outlet with a couple of businesses. With my francs in hand, I ordered some fries, a burger and a bottle of water and sat down to eat. I didn't know it yet, but this would become my favourite place to eat every evening for years to come.

The next few days were all about exploring and finding out what was on offer, while at the same time being naked. The surprising thing, even back in 1994, was this campsite was full of everything one would require. There were at least eight restaurants, a number of clothes shops, mainly selling wraps, a book shop, wine merchants, cake and bread shop, a cinema, tv room, health suite, swimming pool, disco and an outdoor stage for evening performances. The outdoor sports complex was impressive: 2 pitches, an adventure playground, horse riding, and indoor table tennis. Also, as you would expect in a campsite there were a number of toilet and shower blocks dotted around the site. If this was a non-naturist campsite, one would of course expect separate male and female facilities. I hadn't really given the showers much thought, perhaps that's why I was somewhat surprised when I found they were all totally communal. I'd spent most of the afternoon naked on the beach with hundreds of people but for some reason I found showering together with total strangers initially a little strange. Once again for a novice this experience didn't fit with 'normal' as even in the privacy of one's own home, showering was usually a solo activity. It was more than showering as part of a crowd I found odd, it was the closeness and the perceived invasion of privacy. My feelings were not dissimilar to the first encounter of the naturist beach some hours before, I thought this would be an opportunity for a good look. However, it was never going to be like that, everyone could see everyone else, there was no embarrassment or shame and although I'd thought it, no one was having their privacy invaded. This was not sexual in the slightest, and even on my first day

I was beginning to understand what naturism was all about. There was a bond between everyone, an agreement that being nude was totally acceptable, whatever one was doing and whatever could be seen. There was no part of the human body that was rude, off limits or to be ashamed about. Showering up close and personal may seem like a voyeuristic activity, in an odd way, it kind of was, but not how I'd expected it. People were chatting away while they were washing in front of each other, including the intimate areas that would usually be attended to in private. Women were shaving everything that needed shaving and men were washing their penises and bum cracks with precision. I certainly wasn't shy myself, or I wouldn't have been there. I got stuck in and immersed myself in the experience of it all. My body was glowing red from the effects of the sun, and I enjoyed all the attention I was getting as people said how red I looked, in French of course. Even though I was completely alone in a French campsite, totally naked….. with a big smile on my face, I didn't have a care in the world. This was like nothing I'd ever experienced before, and I loved every minute of it. During that first week on the site, I certainly smiled a lot as I soaked in the atmosphere and the culture.

Something I had to try, while at the campsite, was the swimming pool. From the moment I arrived at the site and threw off my clothes it was though I hadn't a care in the world. The experience of the pool would be no different, it just felt so refreshing and so natural to be free of swimming trunks. Exactly like the beach, in the pool no one had a care. There was a toddler pool and a main pool with sun loungers scattered around. There were serious swimmers doing lengths and there were kids just messing around as in any normal pool. I remember seeing a heavily pregnant lady standing by the edge of the water while her partner on the other side of the pool filmed her with a cine camera. At least back in 1994 there appeared to be no rules, no fuss, just total relaxed naturism. Of course, the pool wasn't immune from some of the sights that I had seen on the crowded beach, but I was slowly learning to take such things in my stride. Once you've seen one arse, you've seen a hundred and so over time the novelty of it all disappeared.

Because most of my time during the day was spent naked, obviously a lot of skin was open to the sun and I had not always been thinking of its effects. This meant that on my first visit I had developed some interesting sun burned areas of the body. I had forgotten to cream my privates and in fact most of the area where my pants would usually be, so I had to purchase a bottle of 'after-sun' especially for those delicate areas.

September was a quieter time to be in the camp, especially after the weekend and so by the end of my stay, not many tents remained. Subsequent trips to CHM would be made in July or August when 'busy' would take on a whole new meaning. Apparently throughout the summer season over 100,000 people visit, making the beaches in high season a sea of naked bodies.

Man Holiday

There is much truth to the saying, that all work and no play, makes Jack a dull boy. Given the luxury of choice, no one likes to work and work without a break. Having the chance to stop, to get some rest and recuperation, is without doubt an essential human need. Every time I have bargained with my wife to let me escape for a few days on my own, I have sold it on the idea that I really need a break, so I can keep working at the pace I do. There is some truth to this, but as this seems to work well, it's the line I employ every time. While I am no spring chicken, I am young at heart and make a fair job of juggling family life, a job, a number of village group activities, committees and some serious d.i.y. projects at home, which most people would only leave to a builder. However, to say I need my own time away, some 'me time' to recover from my hard work, would not be entirely accurate. I certainly value time to fully unwind in order to get a different perspective on things, but the truth is, its more about *where* I go that makes the difference. This is because there's no other place I'm drawn to, that if given the chance, would spend my whole summer. While my experiences of being there have given me a sense of finding my own personal utopia, unfortunately the present circumstances mean I keep this entirely to myself. I would love to talk openly about my favourite place, how it makes me feel and the experiences I have, but I can't. This is something I am totally unhappy about and would like to be different, but the reality is, it's unlikely to be. A mere mention of going there as a family or even as a couple is met by a sharp retort. "No way! You are joking aren't you!? You don't really want to do that?" I have no choice but to quickly back down and say, "I was joking, of course I wasn't serious." The problem is an obvious one, it's not like I'm trying to convince my wife to come hill walking with me, to see amazing views. I'm telling my wife how much I really enjoy being naked and furthermore, how there's a particular place in France she could be naked with me, which she would love, if only she'd give it a try. Even as a joke it's a non-starter, so on a serious level it's not something that will change soon. The only feelings that remain, are those of sadness as I am left with little choice but to have my experiences in secret, but it's not the way I want it. If only I could convey this total blissful freedom in some way, if only this feeling didn't come from being naked, perhaps it would be an easier conversation? However, there is no escaping the fact, that it is about being naked, an activity synonymous with being embarrassed or ashamed in normal walks of life...... even indecent, depending on the perspective. As prudish as my immediate family are, even in a European country as relaxed as France, spending the whole time naked is seen as unusual and certainly not the accepted norm. For some, it seems impossible to remove the lewdness and perceived seediness of nudity, from what naturism is. It is as though, being naked in front of others or seeing other people naked, is in some way wrong and there is a lacking in moral standards. Having spent so much time in C.H.M, I feel totally the opposite, and know that any naturist alone, with a partner or as a family would feel odd and out of place, not being naked in such surroundings. Oddly, I can remember a lady, who dressed in a swimsuit, casually walked her dog along the nudist beach. As she did, it was obvious that heads were turning and as strange as sounds, a resident walked past me on the beach and commented in English, "I bet she feels out of place?". It was like everyone was thinking aloud, "What is she doing with her swimsuit on?" I can remember many conversations with other English-speaking holiday makers who shared their story of how they came to be there. The overwhelming similarity, was the agreement on how being nude, was such a refreshing experience. Also, that there were no barriers, hang ups, or rudeness and were amazed how everyone, had a freedom to just enjoy themselves, without a care in the world. While chatting to a father from the south of England recently we both agreed that there is nowhere like it perhaps on the planet and how lucky we felt to be there, to have discovered a piece of paradise. We also agreed that while it was very difficult to talk about this to anyone back home, if they gave it a try, they would soon understand. As we were deep in conversation a very skilled, sandcastle-builder was creating a masterpiece behind us, which became the focus of attention for anyone passing with a camera. He looked up at his son and daughter who were also creating their own less glamourous masterpiece from sand. "Where else, he said, can a family enjoy a place like this with no hang ups and no worries, in total safety?" He was right of course. To the outsider this made no sense, it was odd, but for everyone there, it was where they could be free.

Although this is a family friendly site with a squeaky-clean reputation, my wife has certainly voiced in the past, that she would never be comfortable going to such a place with children. I think this is another reason why any present conversations on the subject quickly grind to a halt. I fail to fully understand her reasoning's behind this and believe it may be partly down to a stereotypical view, that nudity somehow equals sex and therefore is incompatible for a family. However, another reason for my lack of understanding, is the fact that this site has a history between us, and we have done far more than just talk about this in the past. In 2003, C.H.M. actually formed part of a two-day stopover while on a French road trip. She had never experienced naturism before and because of this and my influence, had bravely agreed to a short stay.

We arrived late in the evening and by the time we reached our allotted pitch, it was dark. I recall this being a tricky affair, trying to find the exact pitch by torch-light whilst a nearby naked man offered some unwanted assistance. His nakedness was unusual, as in the coolness of the evening at C.H.M. there tends to be less nudity and people usually dress for evening entertainment. The first night for her up till that point was a relatively easy affair, one naked man and no big shocks. However, things would quickly change as we headed off for a well-deserved shower, after such a long hot day of driving. I guess I never really explained, what it would be like, on the site and although I thought it would take some getting used to, I wasn't ready for her initial reaction. As we arrived at the shower building, she became aware that she would be naked, out in the open, for all to see. Furthermore, there were others at the showers which now meant this usually private function, would be conducted in front of random strangers. By this point she was feeling very awkward, to the point of being quite angry with me. The showers themselves were open-air on the outside of a rectangular structure, five on each side, with one of them being partially covered by a divider. When I pointed out the more secluded shower, she made me stand in front of the opening preventing anyone from looking, then quickly stripped off to have a very quick rinse. The shower block remains to this day and every time I pass it, I can't help thinking back to that first night of our stay on the 12th of August 2003. This was not the best of beginnings, but it did improve following this. When daylight came and we eventually headed for the beach she became totally relaxed only wearing a towel over her shoulder. We experienced the beach together, the pool, and more showers this time openly in front of others, for two whole days, but to this day I wish we had stayed longer as I felt she never really gave naturism a chance. In recent years I have often had the idea that we would include this as, at least, part of our annual family holiday. Part of me so much wants to share this experience and see it as a normal holiday. The reality is while thousands of Europeans do see this as normal, most Brits don't, and my wife won't. This being the case, since we last visited, I have been in secret many times. I can only manage this for one reason, my wife knows that I love swimming and knows that at least once a year I like to go snorkelling or surfing whenever possible. So, over the years, this has become known as my 'man-holiday' where I go away alone to experience the sea for 3, 4 or 5 days. I have been to a campsite close to Biarritz, I have been to Majorca snorkelling but the other times, random campsites which I name before I head off for the French Atlantic coast. This year I have decided to go to the southwest coast of Ireland as there are some great surfing beaches and will remember to pack my wetsuit. Of course, I have never actually been to any of these places, they are just cover stories. There are some years when she scowls at me and says, "I hope you're not just going to a nudist camp on your own?" This affirms that I definitely couldn't let on where I've actually been, but also, she is saying, 'I know you'd like to go'. My worry is getting sun burnt where my swimming shorts are supposed to be and some years that has happened. On return home, I spend the next few days showering with the door locked and get changed quickly in private. Although I think my wife has the idea that I'd take any chance to be naked, it wouldn't necessarily be the case. If my garden was totally secluded and it was a warm day, I wouldn't prefer to be nude. In fact, even if there was a naturist beach nearby, I wouldn't necessarily rush to be naked on it. The truth for me, is that after sampling this particular site in France, and the atmosphere it has, it's the only place where I choose to throw off my clothes. To that end, there is no doubt at all that I have a love affair with that French site. When I'm not there, I imagine what it would be like to be there, especially in peak season. I have to date been twelve times and I'm looking forward to next year being number thirteen…. if I'm lucky enough. I usually decide to go sometime in July or early August, which is a particularly busy time of the year. But exactly how busy, I discovered some years ago to my detriment, when assuming I would easily be able to order a taxi to Lesparre railway station for my return journey. The date was Saturday the 1st of August, which unknown to me was the busiest of the French calendar. It's apparently known as 'Black Saturday' when holiday makers take to the roads and services like taxis are in high demand.

On recent trips I have chosen a flight direct to Bordeaux and hired a car. This has now been the fifth time I've done it this way, as it allows complete flexibility on what I do when I arrive, but importantly, allows me to speed up my arrival time to the site. Since having a car, I have been able to shop using a bank card in the next town or go to a nearby camping resort to get a brochure. Both of these things have been useful, in my story of where I have stayed. Transport has also been essential in my past quests to checkout three other major naturist resorts in France. In 2015 I spent almost two days off site and clocked up over 800k visiting Euronat, La Jenny and Cap D'agde, on the south coast of France. Neither of these was on a par with C.H.M. but Cap D'agde was something different altogether. Over the years the travel alone, has certainly formed part of the overall adventure, especially when faced with deadlines to catch flights or trains. I recall vividly, one year's return journey, which was every bit as exciting as a 'the bourn identity'. The whole journey went wrong from the beginning. There was no taxi available from the campsite, so I had to wait for a bus. When I eventually arrived at Lesparre station, I found that the trains were running on a completely different timetable to the one I'd researched. Eventually, instead of waiting for the train, another bus arrived which by luck was going to Bordeaux city centre where I then hailed a taxi and paid a stupid fee to go just a few miles to Merignac airport. I arrived late and ran to the check-in desk, to be told it was closed but if I had a pre-printed boarding pass, the aeroplane may not have left. No one in the building would print one for me so I ran, sweating and completely out of breath with an enormous bag, through the main airport terminal looking for a helpdesk of some kind. Luckily, I manged to find a kind lady at a car hire desk who logged into the website for me and printed the boarding pass. The flight should have been leaving in minutes. I ran not caring what I looked like, like my life depended on it, back to airport security then on to passport control. The official at the desk, obviously smirking shouted," Woah!" and asked for my passport. I slowed down and handed it over, "bonjour" I said, which of course was the wrong thing, but I was so flustered, I'm surprised I didn't say worse. As I was waved on, I held my passport tight and ran around the corner towards the gate. I quickly found out what the guys' smirk was all about. As I saw the gate ahead of me, I was met by the sight of a que…. full of fed-up looking passengers, who luckily for me had been delayed for half an hour. While this journey was an unusual one, in hindsight over the years, I certainly could have made it easier for myself.

1994- lift to London, train to Newhaven, ferry to Dieppe, train to Paris, TGV to Bordeaux, train to Lesparre, bus to Montalivet.

1996- lift to Waterloo London, Eurostar to Paris, then overnight sleeper to Bordeaux, train to Lesparre, taxi to CHM.

1998- lift to Dover, ferry to Calias, train to Paris, overnight sleeper – rest as 1996.

2003- roadtrip across France, C.H.M. as part of two-day stopover.

2009- flight, train, taxi (return- bus, bus, taxi, flight)
2011- flight, train, bus (return- bus, bus, flight)
2013, 2015, 2017, 2018, 2019- flight, car hire
(2020 and 2021 were non-starters for obvious reasons- covid19)

Before the age of budget air travel, my favourite mode of transport would have been the train..... especially the overnight sleeper. There was something so romantic about catching the Eurostar from London to Paris, then boarding the overnight train that slowly trundled its way, through the night to Bordeaux. I climbed onboard in the summer heat and made my way to the numbered bunk. Travelling second class meant that instead four spacious beds, there were six crammed into each compartment. Even if I had travelled first class, it would have made little difference, as I couldn't remember sleeping a wink. The train pulled into Bordeaux, in the early hours of the morning, leaving almost an hour before the first train north towards Lesparre, which departed around 0800am. The advantage of an early start was a full day at the site, with no more time wasted with travel. The downside, I discovered in 1996, was a vagrant drunk who had not yet woken to the world and had taken up residence in the gent's toilets in Lesparre station. I was so desperate to use the loo, I had to force the door open, as there was a person laying against the other side of it. As I forced my way in, I was somewhat surprised at it being a woman, but after using the loo I came out and she was gone.

Every time I visit that certain campsite in Montalivet, there is always more, than just the feeling of being naked, there's something special about the place itself. Anything to do with C.H.M. is difficult to put into words, unless you have actually experienced it. There is a feeling of acceptance and belonging to something special. It's like, everyone knows that the place is paradise, and they are the only ones who know it. Naturism has its own culture, that is obvious, but to be a resident of C.H.M. in many respects.... as far as I'm concerned, is to be one of 'the elite'. There are people from many different countries, making communication difficult at times but because of the commonality, everyone is so friendly and easy to get on with. Being nude certainly does a lot to help break down any barriers caused by differences such as language, ethnicity and perceptions that clothes cause. The friendliness and atmosphere of this site make it a magical place to be...... but considering the history of C.H.M. ...... maybe it is one of the most *unique* in the world. However, to fully appreciate the beginnings of this place it is useful to grasp the entire history of this activity.

It may be safe to assume, that there have been

many cultures throughout history for which nudity has been a normal pastime. Perhaps the first to be documented, and certainly well-known, were the ancient Greeks and Romans who carried out sporting activities au natural. The historical writings emphasise sports and competition, not the fact that while they were nude, they decided to exercise. However, it was in 1891 in British India when people met together for the purpose of enjoying nakedness which perhaps made this the first naturist club in the world? Some years after world war one, it was Europe that saw the birth of a new 'naked culture'. Germans initially followed by the French, pioneered this healthy outdoor lifestyle seeking fresh air, sunshine and exercise in the nude. This first became popular following the world war in the early 1900's, especially amongst Germans, and attracted socialists, liberals and pacifists. Hitler saw this as potential opposition and made it a state regulated activity. At the same time across Europe, notably France, Germany and the UK.. clubs for those enjoying this leisure pastime sprang up. The largest initially being a club in Hamburg, in 1903. By the 1920's and 30's, this new activity spread from Europe to the United States. Publications soon became available, for those who had an interest in this particular lifestyle. One of the most well-known of these, was the magazine, 'Health and Efficiency formed around 1921, later to be known as 'H&E'. This focused on a healthy outdoor lifestyle which initially, was not *totally* devoted to nakedness. It wasn't until 1931-32 that H&E became entirely nudist and in 1934 advocated that the term nudist, be replaced by naturist and naturism. Interestingly, as naturism was encountered in Europe, it initially met little resistance in terms of it ever being labelled as an unwholesome act. In fact, in 1927 the Dean of St Pauls Cathedral in London declared, "the new freedom of the body, which is sweeping across Europe, is a splendid omen of increasing health". However, this was short lived as three years later, the opening of Vincents Ray sun club in the UK was mobbed by opposition. The 1930's saw the subject of the naked lifestyle brought to the fore, as new publications and advertising campaigns arose on a national scale, namely the 'National Sun and Air Association'(1931) and 'Sun Bathing Review'(1933). In 1943 'The British Sunbathing Society' was formed, and its first general meeting was held with 23 UK naturist clubs in attendance. Eight years later in 1951, the British Sunbathing Association organised an international conference in London, as part of the London Festival of Britain. This was attended by worldwide naturist leaders and lay the foundations for the formation of the International Naturist Federation – INF. This in many respects paved the way for what had already begun in Montalivet, in the creation of the world's first, international naturist resort.

The stretch of Aquitaine coastline where Montalivet is situated, had been noted from before the first world war, as a place where nude bathing had been practiced. Following the introduction of paid annual leave in France, in 1936, Christiane and Albert Lecocq from Arras sought a private site on the beach, which would be known as 'centre heliomarin' which translates to, centre of sun and sea (C.H.M.). They were introduced to the Mayor of Vendays Montalivet who rented them 59 acres of burnt forest, that was zoned to become a holiday resort. Papers were signed on the 23rd July 1950 and the lease was taken in the name of Albert Lecocq, for a non-profit making suburban club. When they first acquired the site, Christaine Lecocq was noted of saying that, "we found total desolation, everything was black or burnt. They had abandoned concrete from the war, five tents and a hut. There was no shade. We went back to the village to sleep on the floor in an open cabin" (cited in British Naturism & Wiki). They had to remove barbed wire and munitions, then cleared a space to build the first wooden bungalows. On 22nd December 1951 a further 62 acres were leased, this time under the name of Federation Francais de Naturisme.

It was fitting that the first world congress of the International Naturist Federation (I.N.F.) was held in Montalivet in 1953, where formal documents were signed and from then on, annual conferences were held in different venues. S.O.C.N.A.T. was formed in 1954 as a separate legal entity, which meant the site was now able to make a profit and in 1956 the site was opened to non-members. Subsequent years saw growth of the site and by 1957, 150 bungalows were available to hire. In 1966 the beach attached to the site became the first official naturist beach in mainland France which helped denote its unique status. By 1968 the total site was now 65 hectares, and the perimeter 6 kilometres, which meant it was now in the record books for being the largest in the world.

One of the first wooden cabins remains on the site, for visitors to step back in time and see what it was like in those early days. There are shelves full of publications on the subject of naturism, mostly featuring C.H.M., and the walls of the cabin contain photos of people building the first huts. After visiting this museum of France's history, for me it added to the emotion of what the site had meant to individuals since the 1950's. In the summer of August 2018, I was lucky enough to meet a resident who had spent many summer months on the site since she was a young girl and was now well into her 60's. She told me that her parents were amongst the first to help build the site back in the early days. This conversation only began after she heard me pass comment to her daughter regarding how really awful the karaoke sounded. To my amazement she was fluent in English and as her mother picked up on this and invited me to their table to eat. This was late in the evening, in the central restaurant area. It turned out that their English neighbours on the site were from Cambridge and had not arrived this year. They told me they were keen to practice their English and so conversation went on. We shared stories of our experiences of the site over the years and the changes we had seen. They asked me how I first found out about the site and I told them about the camping book back in 1994, also about how the site didn't openly advertise, except in the odd naturist magazine. The only other place the beach or parts of the camp have been covered, is in the photographic works of the U.S. photographer Jock Sturgess. The majority of his photographic subjects have been captured with the stunning backdrop of the golden sands of C.H.M. beach – naked of course. Much of his work captures youth and continues into adulthood and beyond. Rather than merely capturing an image, his work emphasises the ongoing relationship with many of his models.

When I mentioned him, they were all surprised?

Not only had they heard of him, but it also turned out they all knew him very well as a close friend on the site and had even been models in some of his published work. I learned that he apparently spends many summer months on the site and can occasionally be seen with camera in hand, usually at dusk on the beach. Some years ago, I was aware that there was an exhibition featuring his work, which included some books for sale and I inquisitively went along for a nosy. I flicked through what was there, as if just to have a quick look around and then leave, as it was late in the afternoon and I was hungry. I made some short conversation with the attendant manning the exhibition.

"I would like to ask him how much of his work was done on this site", I said.

"Who", he replied.

"Jock Sturgess", I said.

"I am Jock Sturgess", was the stern reply.

At the time, I was so embarrassed and apologised profusely. When I told this story to my newly found friends at the table, they laughed more than a little.

Open photography of others on the site is not permitted for obvious reasons of consent and the nature of the captured image. Although in private, people often do take photos of the beach, sea, sandcastles and own family circle without others in the background. Attitudes have certainly changed over the years since 1994, when people would openly snap away without a care. Back then, I even saw professional photographers on the beach with their own female models and assistants helping with equipment. However, these days if anyone openly walks around with any image taking device they could expect to be challenged and so to that end it doesn't happen. The beach and indeed the whole site, is free of any such behaviour which adds to the feeling of safety, innocence and freedom. You really can be totally relaxed and carefree, as you stroll around or lay on the beach. When I think of bringing my wife to C.H.M, I often have a vision in my mind of a man and woman walking along, hand in hand with smiles on their faces, and while I'm dreaming, I also think of Adam and Eve in the garden of Eden, the first paradise, at least before they blew it with that darn apple tree. As I haven't yet seen any apple trees in C.H.M., it remains my paradise, at least on earth anyway.

A few days after my return in the of summer 2018, my sister-in-law asked me if her husband could come on my 'man holiday' next year. I only knew one reply, not that she would take me seriously.

"Do you think he would be ok on a naturist beach?"

"Probably not", was her very matter of fact...... but honest reply.

I'd always thought that I'd quite like to visit with a friend or family member, as the surf and nightlife makes for an exciting time alone. As always, it's the nudity that acts as a deterrent and from what I was told, I should take him off the list of possible companions.

Dare to dream

As with anything in life, you may not know if you like something until you try it. Whether deciding upon a car, moving to a new area or a new job, losing the comfort of what we know and taking a chance on a new thing, can sometimes pay off. I grew up in a village on the outskirts of Ely in Cambridgeshire and so consider myself very much, a southerner. After a number of trips to the Lake District and other journeys north, I thought I might be missing out on something, notably the beautiful countryside. My childhood home was slap-bang in the middle of 'the fens', which is an enormous expanse of reclaimed wetland, drained hundreds of years ago to allow the land to be used for agriculture. The downside for anyone living in the area apart from the endless expanse of crops, is that there are absolutely no hills.

Back in 1989 while on a week's holiday with my local church, I stayed with a group of friends in a Butlin's holiday camp in Skegness, attending an event known as Spring Harvest. There were only a small number of these events held around the country, so each one drew in crowds from, in some cases, hundreds of miles away. It was no surprise therefore to meet a crowd of young people from a small village north of Leeds. They all seemed extremely friendly and a few of us thought that some of the females were especially nice. The idea that northern folk were friendlier than the south was extremely apparent with this group we had met, and so added to the fondness that was growing within, for 'the north'. In the years that followed, namely 1993 and 2000, my attempts at living in the north were very much an anti-climax. Whilst I wasn't afraid of risk, on these occasions, relocating didn't pay off. There certainly was amazing scenery, but I never made the right connections. Feeling lonely and marooned in this northern land I moved home..... twice. Personally, I think these types of experiences are valuable as you go through life. I really do believe that you should do things on a whim, or after having an idea, 'I wonder what it would be like to….'

While recognising that there are people who love to embrace new experiences, others will find the same situations an impossible challenge. Holidays on the most part are quite innocuous and tend to have more advantages than disadvantages, however taking an adventure on a whim seems not to be for every generation. I find it difficult to understand why when people get to midlife and become more aware of their own mortality, are they less likely to try new things. While I may be guilty of making a generalisation, it is not uncommon to hear of a person who finds they have a finite time to live, wanting to take a last holiday or tick as many things off their bucket list as possible. Perhaps as you age, you are able through experience, to pick the good from the not so good and so do the things you know you like? There are some interesting facts around choices of holiday destinations after fifty. It would seem, that the majority after this age prefer to visit the same destination year on year and *not* try something new. It actually makes perfect sense, not to risk a hard-earned break on a venue, holiday company or a new route, that may turn out to be a poor experience. Although I personally struggle to understand this viewpoint. As much as I love the heat from an open fire during the winter months, while the wind and rain howls outside, the summer is my friend. It is when all my winter plans are realised, in every sense. Why become a cliché when you get older? Being inquisitive and having imagination, should always be followed by action. This is the stuff of life not just reserved for the under fifty generation. It's the insecurity of taking a chance, verses not turning the idea into a reality. For me, the juice has always been the visceral reality of the experience itself, whatever it is.

I fully appreciate that giving nakedness a go, somewhere other than one's own home, is somewhat different to trying a new holiday destination. There are some things in life that are so unusual, that the serious thought of trying them wouldn't normally enter your mind. I could put a number of things on this list, like bungee jumping, parachuting, pot holing, or mending a roof. Obviously, most of these have a lot to do with heights and everything to do with my fear, so I will never think of trying them. Although they are not impossible, I would never choose to take a risk and have a go because my choice has been removed by fear. It's quite possible that a number of people may have a fear of trying naturism, although it's likely not to be a fear of nudity, more that of what you think you look like or what others may say. If someone asks you to come to a sauna where no one will be wearing a costume you may say that you have no interest, or you are not that kind of person. An answer like this sounds pretty definite, and would maybe always be a no. However, an answer like, I daren't, I'm scared to, I don't have a good-looking body or what will people think. This is not a no, it's, I would but I feel like I can't because of this reason. Further still you may say, I have no one to go with, I don't know how to, or I've never done anything like that before. These answers now sound like, I'm a little apprehensive but in the right circumstances….. I may be persuaded.

Perhaps there is a different way of looking at the

subject of going naked for the first time. Why do people try abseiling, scuba diving, canoeing, building a wall, driving a digger or even sea fishing? Of course, first they have the idea, that it's …something not been tried before… and they would like to have ago. The reasons may be, for the experience, for the fun of it, to gain a sense of achievement or just to escape the hub-hub of life. After the idea, the steps to these are obvious, carry out some research about where and how, maybe ask other opinions, and then simply give it a try. However, when nudity is thrown into the mix, giving it a try becomes more complicated. I suspect, for most people, naturism never gets further than the idea stage, but assuming it does, it quickly grinds to a halt with… 'what?!!'. The research into the 'where and how' part, is really easy as there are so many choices of venue, whether solo or with a group. Asking around, if anyone knows anything about the subject or where to give it a try is a minefield, as it could be met with any answer, so that's a no-go as well. However, allowing naturism to make it past the idea stage, and being able to consider its merits maybe simpler than you first thought, if only you were able to change perspective. Why is being nude really any different to trying something as innocent as skiing, climbing a mountain or entering a fun run? Although this may be a simplistic view, when it comes down to it, it's merely something new to try out and to hell with the stigma attached. Yet another way of approaching the subject is by going there and giving it a try, as an idea in your mind and see how it sits. For example, close your eyes and take yourself to a hot beach, perhaps alone, first of all. Feel the sensation of the all-over heat, not completely unlike laying in front of an open fire, but instead, open to the elements. If that doesn't work for you, try a warm outdoor Jacuzzi surrounded by palm trees feeling fully relaxed with no worries and no clothes except a pair of sunglasses (as a side note, this is a section of CHM pool near the beach). Once again, this can be private and secluded or it could be with a friendly but totally anonymous group, whatever works for you. If you are able to imagine this kind of scenario and stay there for a while, then you may even be comfortable entertaining 'nudity' as a serious idea. 'Blonde' was certainly right in the lyrics of the song 'dreaming', because it is free, it costs you nothing, and you haven't committed yourself to anything at all. Of course, naturism is certainly not for everyone, if you won't even allow yourself to dream of that beach or secluded campsite then there is little chance that this is for you. As for turning an idea into a reality, even if it's initially a case of mind over matter, the end results far outweigh any objections, you may have had.

Choosing a new thing in life, whatever it is, can be fraught with pitfalls and may not *always* be what you expected. We don't always make choices that are the right ones, as that's an impossible task. Making mistakes, is an inherent human disposition, so phrases like, 'live and learn' or 'learn by one's mistakes' are true for all of us. To some extent, this is what happened to me during my discoveries. Although, it wasn't that I made mistakes, instead my curiosities caused me to encounter new experiences and these in turn changed my opinions. I write this short chapter as a preamble and back-drop to set the scene for my somewhat 'off road' adventures in the coming chapters.

The swims

After my initial visit to Montilavet in 1994, I was curious to what naturist activities may be happening back on home soil. After my initial chance finding of the advert for C.H.M., once again, it was only by chance that I noticed a magazine called 'H&E'. Until that time, I'd never heard of it, it wasn't the title that caught my eye, it was a word on the front cover, 'naturist'. I soon became aware that inside each copy, were a number of pages advertising naturist clubs, naturist swims held in public pools and all sorts of other adverts for holidays, books, videos and even bed and breakfasts for a short break in the nude. There were adverts for nude swims all over the UK, however my first experience would be in a pool just a few miles away. Although I had swam in this pool many times in my youth, on this occasion it was to be very different. I didn't go alone as I was lucky enough to be able to take my girlfriend along with me. She had no reservations prior to the trip and even during the event, she had no hang ups at all and just got on with it. The first thing that struck me, was male or female changing rooms meant nothing. Not knowing this, we initially had entered our own respective changing rooms, but after finding the opposite sex in with me I quickly ran across the adjoining corridor into the female changing room and brought her in with me. Just like France had been some months earlier, this time we both experienced the nervous excitement of our first naturist swim. We did our best to make the completely unusual, as normal as we could.... getting undressed in the wrong changing room, not putting on a costume then walking out into the pool area completely naked, joining everyone else doing just the same. The pool itself was just a standard deep end, shallow end pool with no frills, although they had thrown in some inflatables for a handful of youngsters. I remember spending most of my time swimming up and down not really knowing what else to do, although I did clamber onto an inflatable now and again for a little variety. I was conscious of how she was finding the experience and between lengths of the pool, checked if she was ok. It turns out for her first time trying such an activity, she was more relaxed than I would have ever been, had I not done this kind of thing before. Just like the first encounter of the French beach there was nothing provocative about the experience in the slightest and even afterwards we never spoke about the nudity we had seen in the pool. Although she did make what I thought was a joke during the swim, as a young lady clambered onto an inflatable in front of us, she reached a hand up, covered my eyes and said, "Don't look". As our allotted time came to an end the mostly submerged bodies now showed themselves as they left the pool and headed to their chosen changing rooms. We both rinsed-off together in the same shower space due to the mass exodus and the fact that there were only two showers. After just a minute, I abandoned showering and headed for my pile of clothes just a few feet away. However, as I looked back, I noticed that she was in no particular hurry to get dressed. In fact, she was deep in conversation with a random guy who was quizzing her about her 'first time' and if she had enjoyed it. I remember feeling very proud of her, of how well she had done as she was only nineteen at the time. How naïve was I, it wasn't until sometime later did I consider the fact that if I had been a single guy in the same situation, I would have quite enjoyed a conversation with a very pretty nineteen-year-old, naked in the shower. My naivety had come from a few days of naturism on the Atlantic coast of France and had considered all naturist events to be similar in terms of behaviour. On the whole, any naturist swims I had been to, as advertised in naturist magazines tolerated no lewdness or unacceptable behaviour. That is not to say that I didn't come across some interesting spectacles and meet some equally interesting individuals. Over the five or six years following my initial France trip, I travelled hundreds of miles and visited over a dozen different swim events up and down the country, some only once but others many times.

Essentially a naturist swim event is every bit the same as a conventional swim session, apart from the obvious. But as it is more like a club event, eventually I became aware of the regulars who hung out together, some stayed in the locality and others travelled further afield to other events. The types of people who attend the swims are varied and to some degree can be dictated by the event itself. Some events allow anyone with identification or British Naturism membership, meaning single guys can get in, while other swims will only allow couples and families. However, there are a few swim events that will only cater for couples, no single guys and no one under eighteen. Each swim has its own reasons for what it allows and who is allowed, but sometimes instead of freedom there is a distinct lack of it, quite different to a French naturist beach.

It is true to say that I could tell many stories about my experiences at naturist swims, including obvious motivations of those who attended. Whether men, women, couples or singles it soon became apparent who was there to enjoy the experience and get to know others of a similar mind and those who were only there to look, which I must add were in the minority. On occasion it was fun watching people trying to negotiate an inflatable obstacle course or a group playing volleyball, although that's not the kind of looking I had issue with. There is certainly a fine line between admiring and gazing on the body beautiful in this setting and being an out and out voyeur. As I had discovered on a naturist beach, there was no part of the body hidden from view, it was just naturism. Of course, this was equally apparent during a swim, and especially the case when people clambered around on inflatables. There were some who were completely blaze about the fact that everything was on show and would just carry on as usual standing around having conversation about something totally unrelated. However, there were also those who with smiles on their faces were fully immersed in the activity of scaling an inflatable lough ness monster, as their senses feasted on the experience of it all. This type of fun, or reckless abandon, however one would describe it, certainly wasn't the theme at all swim events I attended, in fact it was the exception. The majority of swims were on the whole, just swimming sessions which were occasionally halted for a drink or snack in the middle. The highlight of most sessions would be the chatter as people got out of the pool, showered and got dressed. Naturist events in the UK are mostly dominated by the over fifty generation, with a handful of younger folk. Some larger swims or pools with more to offer drew in a more balanced clientele, but always with the majority over the age of fifty. This is in no way a negative comment about attendees, but as an observation, this was very different to what I had experienced in France. However, whatever the ages of those who attended, when people came together to share this 'freedom' there was an unspoken unity between them. Their ritual 'throwing off of their clothes' in front of sometimes embarrassed pool lifeguards, made a statement that defined them, even if they weren't immediately aware of it. Although these swim sessions were different in every way to C.H.M. I certainly understood that people were trying to achieve the same thing, even if it was limited to an indoor pool for a couple of hours every month. Some events met at pools, but a few used the whole leisure centre which meant the experience was very different. Instead of the focus being on the water, such events allowed you to wander around and enjoy all the facilities, totally naked of course.

While the experiences of the swims never matched those first four days in France, communication was far easier, as obviously almost everyone spoke English. In France, I didn't necessarily need anyone to talk with about my experience, but back in England I could if I chose to, and I did. It was great to ask people how far they had travelled and how long they had been attending each venue, and over time I got to know, if only by face, some of the regulars. As with any walk of society but perhaps more apparent when linked with nudity, occasionally I stumbled across the unusual and even absurd. I met a couple who were quite openly into swinging and even though this was not the place for them, they were doing their best to attract recruits to meet with later in the evening. I remember on one occasion chatting to what I thought was a couple in their late teens who were chasing each other over an inflatable with the guy taking up the rear with everything to see in front of him, if you get my drift. He was about to fall off and I gave him a push up, and so we made small talk. "Have you come with your girlfriend?" I asked, as it looked the most obvious. "No" he said, "this is my sister". Every now and again, naturism would do that to you. You could look at a situation and think it may be bordering on sexual and then find it wasn't. Also, there were times you would think something wasn't provocative at all and find that some were thinking it was. There were many examples of these types of situations. I always thought that the people who struggled with nudity the most, may have been the pool attendants, who had been rostered on to a shift where the pools occupants were all totally naked. It wasn't uncommon for the young female attendants to be red faced, especially when a naked young man attempted to strike up conversation. Then there were the young male attendants who would be mesmerised as if they had never seen a naked girl before. Actually, the truth for most attendants was that they had probably never come across such a diverse selection of people of all ages, totally nude. For myself, being naked in the pool was never a sexual experience, much the same as a naturist beach, it couldn't be further from it. Although I often wondered how the lifeguards found it and perhaps was a conversation, I wish I had had. However, before I portray myself as completely innocent, there was one situation when I thought I was going to be embarrassed by a bodily reaction. While still in my early 20's I attended a naturist swim with a sauna on the side of the pool. I jumped out of the pool into the sauna which started to rapidly fill, with more and more bodies piling in. There was no space left for gaps between touching thighs and with some sitting on laps who weren't so heavy. Then it happened. I did my best to change the subject in my head and distinctly remembering the line from the Austin Powers movie, 'Margaret Thatcher on a cold day!' I stayed for a while but in the end had to bail out while I could. To this day I put it down to an involuntary body reaction due to the heat and touching bodies rather than a sexual thought. Apart from my own secret near miss, I was never aware of anyone in the state of arousal or deliberate lewdness. While there may have been the very odd male with steamed up goggles, on the whole there was no touching, no open depravity, and no one being taken advantage of. Officially organised naturist swim sessions throughout the UK are for experiencing the wholesome activity and freedom of naturism, with an emphasis on enjoying the social interaction it provides. Every 'swim' seems to make a conscious effort in statement and in the way it monitors how members act, to reinforce acceptable behaviour. Nevertheless, throughout the years of experiencing nude swims, I personally felt these were a tainted version of the naturism I had first discovered.

Secret Excursions

Since my first encounter in Montilavet in 1994, I have made a number of special trips, diversions or secret excursions in order to experience a number of naturist venues. Whilst I may have travelled the best part of a day to reach some destinations, the longest I have ever stayed is just a few hours, each destination being a rekey for a possible future vacation.

The summer of 1999 was the year I met my future wife in the car park of a shopping centre in Calais. It wasn't that we'd had met randomly while shopping, it was because I'd decided against the channel tunnel from Folkestone to Calais and had taken a ferry instead. It's a difficult one to explain, but the fear of being stuck in a long tunnel underground and flying are similar, so as there was a boat available, I took that option. This meant, that the driver of the coach had to make an unplanned stop before continuing on to Pineda de Mar in Spain situated around 40km north of Barcelona. It was exciting meeting a new bunch of people on holiday, but especially fun getting to know one particular young lady. Although we didn't realise it at the time, the future held a lifetime together, with any luck.... The holiday included a number of group excursions, some of which I went to, others I chose to opt out of. When the group of around 40 or so hopped on a coach for a daytrip to Barcelona, I decided to do my own thing. Instead of travelling with the group, I took the coast line south as the trains were very good value and the scenery, stunning. There were great views of the harbours, beaches and the people on them. Although I was excited about my first trip to Barcelona and everything it had to offer, I soon became aware of another distraction. I had not considered Spain or indeed any other country to be as open as France, how naïve was I?... As the train journeyed south, I began to see singles and couples and then whole beaches carpeted with nudity. I spent the day in Barcelona as planned but this discovery meant there was now a destination for future trips in years to come. However, I didn't let the holiday go by before I took a short train ride to one of the nearest beaches where I had spotted some nude folk a few days earlier. This would have been my third naturist beach venture and certainly the shortest skinny dip ever. As if I was carving another conquest on my bedpost, I discarded my clothes and dived straight into naked freedom. This wasn't an official beach and only noticed one other person some way off doing the same. I was in the sea for maybe only three minutes and spent an equal amount of time on the sand before covering up. My return journey, which involved almost a mile a mile walk back to the nearest station, was consumed with thoughts of foolishness. There had been little point in what I'd done, and the lack of time spent there had made it worse.

In 2001 I went alone on a similar group holiday to a camp site in Playa D'aro also on the Costa Brava coast around 60km north of Barcelona. This area was totally unknown to me, but the campsite had an internet café which allowed me to carry out some research. There was a popular naturist beach some miles to the north but disappointingly was totally inaccessible. There were no nearby train links, and buses were not much better, leaving a walk of around 3km. Playa D'aro has some stunning beaches immediately of the north of the town and boasts some of the most picturesque coves in Spain, which are ideal for snorkelling. Given a choice between a wide-open beach and secluded coves, I'm a coves man all day long. So, if there was one thing that could be improved with C.H.M. if I dare say such a thing, it would be the beach, but this of course is only my personal view. I spent a week snorkelling and walking the rocky cliff path to my hearts' content. Being naked would have been a bonus but this beach on its own, was enough. Although at the back of my mind remained this mystery beach some 15km to the north, just out of reach and to make things worse, I was almost out of cash. I did my best research, literally counted my pennies and took a gamble. I walked out of the campsite early one afternoon and along the road to where I had seen buses picking up passengers. All I knew, was the name of the nearest village and the name of the beach; I knew no Spanish and had no map. Pretty much anything could go wrong, and I would be stranded with no one to contact for help. I had only been walking for a few minutes and was already feeling quite overcome with the heat. Once again, I was setting off on an insane journey to somewhere or nowhere, and I considered turning back. However, a bus arrived, and I showed the driver the village and beach name 'Platja de illla Roja', he had worked out that I was English and said, "Yes, get on". The bus actually took me closer than expected, to a small beach car park with a path leading off over a hill to the north. I didn't notice the heat as I inquisitively headed off down the path which could have been leading in totally the wrong direction for all I knew, as there were no signs. After ten minutes I became aware of an outcrop of rock and a beautiful little beach hidden away under the cliff path. A path carved out of the rocks led steeply down to the beach with the words 'naturista', painted in white on the rocks. As if I was missing out on something, I hurriedly headed down to the beach. There were maybe a hundred naturists enjoying the absolute tranquillity, seclusion and hot sun. I found a spot smack in the middle of them all and disrobed. By 2001, this was the most beautiful standalone naturist beach I had found and was completely unexpected. Apart from the concern of the return journey, there was every reason to stay on the beach as long as I could, so I spent a good couple of hours soaking up the sun and atmosphere. The sea was calm and warm, in fact the cove was as picturesque as any holiday brochure. There was a balance of ages on the beach, similar to France and everyone respected everyone else. Although out of the blue, a guy directly in front of me lifted his expensive looking camera with a wide angled lens and pointed it at a young woman sitting not six feet away from him. As he did this, a nearby man voiced his concern loud enough for the woman to look up. It was as if she knew how beautiful a picture she would make and swept her hair away from her face nodding towards the master at his work. Her pose left nothing to the imagination, and he snapped away while those around jealously looked on. After a perfect afternoon on the beach, I reluctantly began the short walk back to the beach steps, only to be interrupted by a naked lunatic. All kids love rock climbing but this fool of a girl instead of walking the beach path had decided to climb straight up the rock, which was some 40ft of a climb. It was so foolish that she drew a small crowd, from not only the naturist beach but also from the pathway above. Luckily, she made it, otherwise the news reports from any accident may have been both comical and tragic at the same time. As I'd had enough excitement for one day, I walked back along the cliff path to search for a bus. It turned out that the bus didn't call at the same spot late in the afternoon and I had a long walk back to the next nearest bus stop. After some time waiting, I chatted with a bus driver who told me that no buses were going my way. For the life of me I can't remember how, but I managed to hitch a lift back to the campsite even though the driver wasn't going in that direction. With a smile and an inner monologue, 'you'll not believe where I've been', I reacquainted myself with the group back at the campsite.

During the summer of 2002 I found myself at a loose end one afternoon while staying with a friend in London for a few days, and so found myself on yet another adventure. I'd heard about a well-known naturist club just outside London and thought I would try to reach it. At the time I had no car and was totally reliant on public transport. Luckily there was a railway station nearby my destination leaving only a mile or two to walk. I had a piece of paper in my pocket with the name of the road I would

find the club on. I found it easily and headed up the steep road towards the clubhouse. I met a gentleman who quoted me a price to come in for the day and showed me around the clubhouse and the gardens. Following this, I continued to explore alone but quickly became disappointed and overwhelmed by a sense of anti-climax that I had wasted my time. If this was a typical naturist club on a hot summer's day in the peak of holiday season, then I wanted out. I found no atmosphere, no conversation, no friendliness, a distinct lack of people and without uttering a word to anyone I made a hasty retreat along the road and back to the station. It was while I was walking that I had one of my hair brained ideas......
and so I'd decided that the days' excursions were not over yet.

In under an hour I was back in London and within the next hour I was walking out onto the street in Brighton. Perhaps one of the most well-known, or should I say publicised, naturist beaches on the south English coast was worth a visit. I knew it was at the far end of the beach near the marina and set off along the seemingly endless promenade. There now was the realisation that I had devoted most of my day attempting to find some 'outdoor' British Naturism, and I hoped that this would not disappoint. The naturist beach could not be seen, as it was hidden from view by a pile of beach stones to the rear and to the sides. There were a couple of signs that made it clear that no clothes were permitted beyond the clearly, manmade barriers. As I entered the area, I could see there was no more than thirty people aged between 40 to old. It had to be said, this was not much different to the club I had visited some hours previous. Instead of liberating freedom, there actually seemed to be an air of awkwardness, or what might even have been called embarrassment. People seemed to keep themselves to themselves and any attempt at conversation didn't get much of a response. On the completely overcrowded train home, while feeling somewhat disappointed, I decided that any future naturism would be on foreign soil.

In 2005, married but before children, we attended an extended family holiday in Spain on the now familiar stretch of coastline near Lloret de Mar. We hired a large people carrier and spent the week touring beaches and popular tourist attractions. Before the holiday, I had secretly done as much homework as I could in terms of where all the nudist beaches were along the nearby beaches. Although there were a number to choose from, I tried to work out from memory where I had seen the largest expanse of naked bodies. This would have been from memory, six years earlier, while the train travelled along the coastline, so getting this right was more luck than judgement. Eventually when the venue of the family outing wasn't entirely something I wanted to do, I made my excuses and stole away in the car for a couple of hours. I remember having a lot further to drive than expected and realising this, drove as fast as I could while using a paper map on my knee. I may have broken a speed limit or two as I travelled south, well over 50km to my destination. When I finally arrived at Arenys de mar there was little time before I was expected back, and so hurried to the beach. After carrying out the act of obligatory nudity, I strolled off along the busy beach. There were a mix of ages, but couples were certainly the majority. As hurriedly walked along, I noticed that almost all of the women were completely hairless. I couldn't be sure if this was a local trend or just a Spanish thing but nevertheless there it was. Furthermore, I couldn't ever remember walking along a beach where the women seemed to lay around, very unladylike, as if they were showing off the latest fashion between their legs. It was either that or they were going for a true all over suntan. I ended up staying for around 30 mins, walking the length of the beach at least twice and having a swim. The beach was mostly sand with one rocky outcrop that would have almost divided the beach in two when the tide came in. The beach had a bar with food available where sun loungers could also be hired which strangely seemed to be frequented by both naturists and those who chose not to be. I wanted to stay, to experience more, but I couldn't I was under pressure to return to my marooned family many miles to the north. I ran to the car and this time drove even faster on the return journey to be reacquainted with some unimpressed family members.

Some years later in 2012, because of my love of the Costa Brava coves, we visited the resort of Cala Gogo just outside Platja d'Aro. The beach had not lost any of its magic and as a bonus even had a small naturist beach just a few coves away. Although the cove was stunning, unfortunately there were only a handful of brave souls going 'all the way'. At the end of our week's holiday, we had booked a hotel for the night in Barcelona. This was for no other reason than a combination of early flight times and returning car hire with young children, made things complicated. In hindsight we should have just ditched the car hire and flown home, even if we had arrived home in the middle of the night, but on this occasion we didn't. On arrival to the hotel, our youngest still in a pram was tired and it was decided that we would wait before going out. This meant there was some time to kill, and I very foolishly asked if I could go for a short drive to the immediate south of the city. Reluctantly she allowed me to go, and I promised not to be long. In many ways this was a mirror of

2005 as I frantically drove around the city searching for a road north back to Arenys de mar, some 25km away. It took much longer than expected to reach the beach and because of this I only stayed for ten minutes. After my annual nudity craving had been met, I jumped in the car and raced back to the hotel. I knew I had taken too long, and in the panic to get back I made a stupid mistake. I drove the UK way round a roundabout and headed up a dual carriageway slip road the wrong way to meet a shocked motorist heading towards me flashing his headlights. I began to feel very stupid indeed, nearly causing an accident over attempting to reach a nudist beach, what kind of idiot was I?

I arrived back at the hotel so late that my wife didn't speak to me for two hours. The children were also very hungry, as we had intended to travel into the city for food ...... the delay was totally my fault. Eventually, after sitting on the pavement of 'Las ramblas' eating McDonalds, due to the lack of benches, she began to speak to me. I vowed never to act so stupid again, to her and myself. The fact that this had impacted on our family holiday was reason alone to come to that conclusion. After all my secret excursions, both at home and abroad, there was a realisation that I should have been satisfied with what I already knew. In most cases, I wasn't at any of these venues for more than a few minutes, but it was enough time to know they weren't the same. I'll always stand by my view that experience is a good thing, but perhaps I also need to concede, that in some respects I failed. In as much as, by 2012 I failed to find anywhere even close to the experiences in had in Montalivet.

Two Days off Site

I left my tent in C.H.M. and headed for the beach, through the now very well-known paths and roads, past the fun pool with its flumes, past the restaurant and bike park towards the lifeguard's observation tower. I carried with me, a nylon lightweight sports sac held closed with a long drawstring which also doubled as a shoulder strap as it was carried. Inside I had a tea shirt, shorts, a two-litre bottle of water, sun cream, sun hat, a bread roll and two large slices of ham bought just a few hours before. I only spent a few minutes sitting on the beach breathing in the tranquil atmosphere before standing and purposefully walking north in the direction of Montilavet les Bains public beach. It was an extremely warm day, which at a guess would have been around 35c, and my back was feeling hot. As it was mostly quite difficult to creams one's own back, the sensation I was feeling was almost certainly untreated burning skin. I took the flimsy bag off my shoulders, dug out a tea shirt and a cap for good measure and put them on. Up until that point I had been enjoying nakedness, while walking towards the edge of the nudist beach. Although there is a substantial wooden sign making it clear what mode of dress is expected either side of it, the beaches inhabitants seem to treat it more as a suggestion than the rule. I stayed nude in a similar way to those who flouted the rules, apart from my cap and tea shirt, for as long as I dared. As I was nearing a busy beach and fast about to become the novelty streaker, I pulled on a pair of shorts and avoided any unwanted attention. Feeling very overdressed, I walked past the surf school and public beach until it began to quieten down again. The area wasn't a nude beach, so I stayed as I was and carried on. I walked what must have been around 3k and stopped. I was very warm indeed and dripping with perspiration. I looked back towards C.H.M. beach but it was gone, nowhere to be seen in the hazy distance. In fact, I had now gone so far that only one person could be seen anywhere. I dropped my bag to the floor and hastily opened the water. As I gulped down the warm liquid, it began to dawn on me that this walk, this mission I was on, was not a clever one. I had only walked a relatively short distance but was desperate for a rest, out of the hot sun.

In the months leading up to this particular man-holiday to Montalivet, I had worked out, using google maps, that it may have been possible to walk along the beach approximately 5km to the next naturist beach and resort,'Euronat'. On my initial visit to Montalivet in 1994 I was aware that as I travelled towards the site on the bus there were other naturist resorts nearby. In fact, as you turn left at the crossroads onto l' avenue de Europe where C.H.M. is situated, there is a sign for Euronat. Although I had discovered and experienced the world renown C.H.M, I had also wondered what other naturist resorts would be like.

My chosen mission was maybe some 2km further along the beach, although by now I was seriously asking myself what I was doing. I was alone in the heat, so my thoughts were spoken out loud to myself. "What am I doing this for? What am I hoping to find? … more naked people? I must be crazy!" For all I knew I had literally walked away from the most idyllic naturist beach in France, in an attempt to compare the one next door. On the face of it, it made no sense and strangely due to my dizzy exhaustion the only thought that came to mind was the phrase or perhaps it's a song, 'mad dogs and Englishmen go out in the midday sun'. This summed it all up perfectly, no more needed to be said. I decided not to pass out in the heat but to turn back and return to familiar surroundings to live another day. I would get to Euronat and two other resorts, but not that year.

Everyone I had seen, either at a swim event in the UK or a naturist beach were obviously there because it was something they enjoyed doing. I began to realise that there was no right or wrong way to enjoy naturism, it was personal in terms of the venue and who it was shared with. By 2012 especially after my fruitless journeys in Spain, my own preferences were becoming clear in terms of the one 'resort' I had visited. Although in complete contradiction, the only thought that remained was that of other resorts across Europe that may be similar to C.H.M. As before, there were not many thoughts in my mind that were not acted out in reality. So, in 2015, after much research and even more anticipation, I had hired a car and was ready for naked adventure. In the months leading up to the journey, I had discovered two resorts within an hour's drive of Montalivet, Euronat and La Jenny. There was also, what could only be described as 'a naturist town' on the south coast near Montpellier, that I'd wanted to visit for many years. As this resort was significantly larger than C.H.M. I'd decided that this should be a holiday, and not just a day trip. The only trouble was, that by the time I had attempted to book a pitch at the resort's campsite, they were fully booked. Not knowing it was so popular, I had simply left it too late and so the holiday was off. However, I was so determined to visit, I'd made plans to do it as a day trip, and so that's what I did. I had all the road routes planned and printed out to take with me, which I had secretly stowed in my luggage.

In 2015, I arrived on site in Montilavet at around 3pm with a real old banger of a hire car just ready to be sold on, which is probably why they threw in a sat-nav as a freebie. I set up tent as usual and headed down to the beach to experience the first nudity of the year. I was met by something new. Although it happens a few times a year, the sandcastle competition was, as yet unexperienced. There was a mixture of abilities, made up of individuals and family groups. Some looked like complete professionals out for nothing else than a win. There were sole artists doing their stuff, and a number of family groups making a team effort. There were marked out pitches with around 15 teams and individuals doing their best. At the far end of the pitches was a table where two staff were taking participants names, while at the same time manning the stopwatch. An English family were adding finishing touches to a quite impressive looking car and they took turns posing for photos, for what must have made for an interesting holiday photo album. Although photos would be a nice to remember the fun of what it was like to be there, I found over the years that memories alone were enough, and equal to any photo album.

As always, I enjoyed every moment of the first day but was keen to set off early on my adventure south and made sure I put my head down early. During the night it began to rain, which is not unusual and in fact when snug in a tent, it can be quite a comforting sound. However on this night, the thud, thud, thud of raindrops was getting louder and louder with an increasing tempo. The tent was only a few years old and so I was confident that I would remain dry, even while my sandals were floating outside in a pool of water. It wasn't until I saw them floating, did I become aware that my tent was pitched in a dip in the ground with nowhere for the water to escape. The ground sheet began to take on the form of a waterbed and areas without my weight on, were visibly now raised from the ground. I took a peek under my foam ground mat and noticed a pool of water, there was a leak! Eventually the rain subsided and there was comparative quiet, apart from the noise from the waves beyond the dunes. Initially I couldn't be sure what it was, but there was a sound, a roaring, which got louder and louder until eventually it hit land. Within a few minutes, storm force winds hit the campsite taking most small tents in its path. My inflatable tent didn't stand a chance and folded around me. Somehow, I found a torch and scrambled out, towards the safety of my car parked next to the tent, which luckily, I had left unlocked. That year I'd only packed shorts, and although I covered myself with a number of tea shirts I had left in the car, it was nowhere near enough to keep me warm.

As a result, I spent most of the night awake from the cold, which was an unusual phenomenon. The plan to set off early and drive to the south coast all before midday, was in tatters. I was tired out from the night's events and without venturing outside it appeared that my tent had disappeared completely. Although by mid-morning after I'd had enough sleep, I stepped outside to find it wrapped around the front wheel of the car. I spent the day resting, rebuilding and making sure everything was ready for the trip south.

After a much-improved sleep, I set off on the 537km journey south to Cap d'Agde. As I had the sat-nav, the printed maps were not required and I made my initial estimates at how long the journey would take. For the most part this was uneventful, although to arrive in good time, I was conscious that keeping a constant speed was of the upmost importance. Toulouse will forever be imprinted on my memory, as it was the point that I managed to get lost even with a sat-nav and in my effort to make up time, was then caught by a speed camera. However, there was no time to dwell on this and around two hours later, had arrived at Cap d'Agde. Although I had a detailed print out of how to get to the 'naked city', I chose to explore the area before reaching my destination. The town had a harbour which separated the naturist quarter from the rest of the town, but there was also a naturist beach beside the main town beach. I decided to drive straight to the town beach and went until I could go no further, accept to enter an oversubscribed car park. As people were driving up and down eagerly looking for a space that didn't exist, I made an illegal double park and ran to the beach. I stood only for one minute looking up and down, trying to get my bearings from the satellite images I had seen. For the most part, this was a normal south of France busy town beach, and I guessed that it would take some time to explore this side of town, to find out exactly where I was. I jumped back in the car to avoid the certainty of a parking ticket and retraced my steps. After a mile or so I came across a road sign which left no ambiguity and directed me towards the naturist quarter. According to the satellite images it looked like it may have been possible to walk across some wasteland to the naturist beach, which would have avoided payment. In reality, it was very overgrown, extremely hot and there were security cameras everywhere, which meant this idea never got off the ground. Instead, I joined a que and after around 15 minutes, showed my passport and paid twenty euros for a day's pass. I was in.

As I had expected to take the scenic route through the adjacent wasteland to the beach, I didn't have a clue where to go or what to expect entering the complex. First things first, shorts, tea shirt and pants off, stuffed them into my rucksack and I was off. Buildings, roads, junctions, shops, hotel, clubs, the place was enormous. I had to ask directions a number of times until I could be sure of the correct route to the beach. My final instructions led me to what had obviously at some point been a smart shopping mall, but now appeared run down and dated. There was a very small supermarket and a number of shops, some of which appeared to sell kinky outfits, leather and whips etc. As I walked on, I noticed a small pool area beside the mall. I recognised this from some naturist literature and film I had seen while researching Cap d'Agde, however the area looked unused and again somewhat tardy. I walked on until I saw the famous or perhaps infamous Heliopolis complex, which instead of the height of summer, looked like it was shut for the winter. I hadn't yet reached the beach, but on appearance alone, this 'naturist city' as it was known, was somewhat of a let-down. I hoped the beach would be an improvement and optimistically stepped from ash felt onto the hot soft sand. The harbour wall could be seen off to the right denoting the end of the naturist area while to the left there seemed to be a beach bar / café. The beach was certainly the busiest I had ever seen with maybe around 2500 bearing themselves to the Mediterranean sun. I walked the length of the beach, first to the harbour wall then back towards the beach café area. I didn't know it yet but the area I had walked was the 'family friendly' area, although oddly for a naturist beach, apart from some at the water's edge there were hardly any families to be seen. The beach café / bar area looked somewhat enticing and decided after my exploration to pay it a visit. As I walked past the bar and followed the shoreline, the beach activity changed. I didn't need to look twice as it was quite clear what this area of the beach was all about. I had heard that there was a seedier side to Cap d'Adge but nothing could have prepared me for things I was about to witness. While people were casually swimming in the sea, not yards away on the beach, couples were laying together casually fondling each other's intimate areas. As I continued to walk further back from the shoreline the sights became more and more bizarre and by now was strictly 'adults only'. When researching Cap d'Adge, I had read a number of reviews and now every one of them were now being played out for real. Without going into detail, pretty much every sex act could be seen, nothing was off limits and at the same time very publically on display. Things were both surreal and strangely amusing at the same time; every few minutes there would be loud screams as individual's sexual enjoyment came to an end, this was followed by cheers and clapping from onlookers. Although curious….. after witnessing this hedonistic behaviour for a few minutes, I had seen enough. I knew Cap d'Adge had an adult beach, which while I was there, had every intention of seeing, however I now began to see how this influenced the whole complex. Although the adult beach was separate, the adult theme was apparent in other parts of the resort and in total contradiction to what I'd been used to in C.H.M. some 500km away. There was something different about Cap d'Adge and it wasn't until I'd ventured on to the adult beach, did I work out what it was. There is not a seedy side to naturism, there never has been. It is based on innocence and freedom of enjoying fresh air without clothes. Whether sunbathing, swimming, or pursuing other activities, sex and arousal is never part of it. So, when sex hungry singles and couples are part of a general family friendly naturist resort, the two won't mix as they are not the same. I walked back to the beach café for a cool drink and some shade, and while I was there chatted to a French guy who could have easily passed as English, if it wasn't for his accent. We discussed the beach and its sights and quickly agreed on the madness of it all. After refreshment, I took a final brisk walk to the harbour wall and then back through the complex and became aware of more adult themed bars and clubs. It was now early evening, and some of the nightlife seemed to be starting early, as people could be seen walking around in provocative underwear and leather gear. I now understood why there were so few families compared with C.H.M; this was certainly a tainted version of the naturism I knew. I was glad to have experienced this site, as it was one to tick off the bucket list, but at risk of seeing more of the same, I got dressed, exited the complex and walked back to my car. I left Cap d'Adge at around 8.45pm and made the long drive back to Montalivet. A tank and a half of fuel and 537km later I was back on the Atlantic coast in C.H.M. Although absolutely exhausted, I smiled and sighed with relief as I unzipped my tent. The smell of the pine trees and the uncomfortable sponge mattress welcomed me back home, and I drifted off to sleep in minutes.

I awoke with a sense of relief, back in my tent, 'normal naturism' and no shocking encounters to stumble upon. I had planned the day ahead to be an easier one, there were two more resorts to tick off my list but this time they were just a few minutes' drive away. Euronat was first, as it was closer, some 5km as the crow flies. I hadn't intended to visit the resort itself, just really to compare the beach. I drove along the coast road, away from Montilavet les Bains sea-front buildings, until I met with the boundary wall of Euronat. My intention was to walk from the road, down onto the beach and then along until it becomes 'naturist' in the same way that someone would with C.H.M's beach. On approach, I realised I was totally unprepared as I had no bag, just the clothes I was wearing. I took a gamble and left a neat pile of clothes, including car keys on the beach and walked on. I had high expectations from resort number two on my list. Opened in 1968, this quickly became the largest camping / caravan, naturist holiday resort in France. The total size including beach, is a staggering 830 acres, making C.H.M. Monta seem comparatively tiny at a mere 400 acres. Even while walking the beach, I began to get a sense of the enormity of the site, but there was something strangely different. It was almost midday, admittedly not usually the busiest time of the day on the beach, but there couldn't have been more than 50 people on it. As I walked along, I noticed a track leading off to the site and inquisitively headed in that direction. The path from the beach met another wider and longer path which seemed to go on for ever through the forest. Eventually I came across a cul-de-sac of wooden chalets, which I had expected to lead to a more central area, but this did not happen for some time....road after road, junction after junction, more and more holiday homes. As I walked, it was dawning on me that the site was enormous. Apart from a relatively small camping and caravan area, the site seemed to consist mostly of chalet style buildings which seemed newer and larger than those at C.H.M. On reaching a central commercial area with shops and a swimming pool, I had been walking for some time and was exhausted. However, there was another feeling which now equalled the exhaustion, as strange as it sounds, I felt naked. I had expected to just blend in, as one would in any naturist site. However, oddly almost everyone I saw was dressed, to the point of actually questioning if I'd somehow walked into the wrong resort. It wasn't a cold day at all and there appeared to be no obvious reason to wear clothes, nevertheless it seemed to be the on-site culture. As an alien in a foreign land, I accepted the way things were but also began to feel quite vulnerable. I felt like I stood out like a sore thumb, as an obvious non-resident. As I began to find my way back to the beach, I memorised names and areas of the site which I also put a number to. If anyone challenged me, I would have been able to quickly recite my fictitious on-site address. The feeling of being asked what I was doing on the site intensified as I reached the main beach entrance I'd intended to use as an exit. Eventually, breathing a sigh of relief, I walked past beach security as the path opened onto the beach. What I didn't know at that time, was as a C.H.M. resident, I had just needed to show my camp pass at the main gate and for a small fee I could have had a bona fide day in Euronat.

By now the beach had a few more participants but still no more than a hundred. Feeling literally and metaphorically naked I walked away from the resort, really hoping my clothes and car keys were still where I'd left them. Luckily, I had avoided the mother of all embarrassments as put on my clothes and left the beach.

As I walked back to my car, I couldn't help comparing Euronat with C.H.M. as they seemed a world apart. Admittedly I had only briefly walked through the site, to the centre and back out again but I found the lack of people difficult to explain. Perhaps as the site was so enormous it was difficult to get a sense of how many people were there? Perhaps it was something to do with the time of day and everyone was having lunch? Perhaps there was some large onsite event taking place which took account for a large group of people not being there? Whatever the reason for the lack of people on site, the effect was a distinct lack of atmosphere. There were times during the afternoon that the central shopping area was quiet at C.H.M. but that was because everyone was on the beach. The opposite, meant at times the beach was quiet, but this was because it was morning and people were at the market, the shops, having lunch or at keep fit. Whatever the time of day, I never felt like there was a lack of people, or lack of atmosphere. C.H.M. was not as large in area but it did appear to have more residents.

After getting back to the car, I felt like heading back to my much-loved C.H.M. but instead headed south to my final destination, La Jenny. This took around forty minutes to reach, through mostly forest lined roads. On arrival I showed my pass to the receptionist an explained that I was staying at CHM; for a small fee I'd acquired a day pass. This resort was on a much smaller scale to CHM, but very similar in the way it had a central restaurant complex. In fact, the central area also included a shop, large pool and restaurants all in one. There was no direct beach access, and a short non-naturist walk was required to reach it. The beach was first on my La Jenny checklist, so I hurriedly made my way through the forest, out into the scorching heat of the afternoon sun. A boardwalk took me over the brow of the dunes until I reached the burning hot sand and although this was the time to remove sandals, it was impossible without burning my feet. As I awkwardly walked through the soft beach sand, the beach came into view. Although the campsite was impressive enough, there were no more than 10 people on the beach, which was quite surprising. If the beach lacked atmosphere, the site itself hadn't lacked character, especially in the central area where everyone seemed to gather. The site also seemed to respect naturism values, as almost everyone wore no clothes. After two days travelling and visiting these new sites, although on a much smaller scale, La Jenny was the only site which came close to the atmosphere of CHM. Although I had high expectations of the experiences I would have on my travels, I think deep down, I never really expected to find somewhere to match my favourite place. As in the past, time spent chasing naked experiences, led to nothing but disappointment. There are a number of naturist resorts around Europe, but at present I am in no hurry to visit these, if only to compare them with what I consider to be the best site in the world.

The Shock of the Nude

There are many occasions in life where nakedness is a must, not because it's something you want to try out, because it makes sense. Apart from the stereotypical teenager who needs encouragement to wash, most of us enjoy the feeling, the relaxation and perhaps the solitude of a shower or a bath. This activity is not rude or provocative; at least it seems unlikely that anyone would avoid washing due to their nakedness, unless someone is watching. Although the fear of being seen, of what people might think, is probably the most common reason why people choose to keep their clothes on. If no one can see, then there is no one who can have an opinion, and no one to cause you to think about what you are doing. The ways in which people react to nudity is a complicated subject, so much so, that some never go further than being naked in the bathtub or for procreation. If we stay with the scenario of the bathtub, I've found by asking just a handful of people that there are a variety of differences. Even on a very warm day, my wife will exit the bath or shower and immediately cover up with a large towel, and that's well before exiting the bathroom itself. This seems to have nothing to do with her upbringing, as her father is known to openly walk around in the altogether between bathroom and bedroom. I discovered this to my amusement back in 2003 while holidaying in Scotland with the extended family. Although she doesn't lock the bathroom door and has no problem with anyone else in the family coming in for a chat, she has always appeared to be out of her comfort zone without at least a towel afterwards. Then there is the question of how long to stay in a towel or when to put clothes on after the bathroom. These answers even in my small anecdotal study range from, 'until you are dry, then get dressed', to 'as long as no one can see, stay nude as long as you want', to 'after a bath we get dressed when we feel like it, there are no rules'. Of course, in the family home, there are no reasons to label anyone as a naturist just because a person takes too long to get dressed, or to suggest that nudity is a problem if it goes on too long. There are those who are happy making breakfast in the altogether, but who wouldn't dream of being in the same state on a beach. It simply comes down to, are you ok with it and is everyone who sees it, ok with it.

There are surprisingly few rules around nakedness in the UK, however according to a couple of well-known TV presenters, the Brits are far from relaxed about the whole subject. Instead of having a take it or leave it, do whatever ever you feel comfortable approach, we seem in this country to be plagued by hang-ups. Well known presenter Kate Humble (Mirror newspaper, June 1997) suggested that she was most comfortable when naked and added that when spending time in her French holiday home, she hardly ever wears clothes. Furthermore, she said that British people seem to be 'obsessed' with nudity in a 'weird and unhealthy way'. Similarly, Ester Ranzen, TV presenter since the 1970's explained in a newspaper article (mail online, Feb 2019) that 'we buttoned up Brits need to chill-out about nudity'. So, is the reaction to nudity purely cultural? Maybe we react in surprise and horror because of our Britishness? This was certainly the case back in 1040AD when Lady Godiva, wife of the Earl of Mercia, challenged her husband to release its people from poverty by reducing taxes. His response was to laugh, saying he would only do this if she rode through the streets naked on horseback, which as history tells us, is exactly what she did. It seems that this was so shocking that after almost a millennia, she is instantly remembered for her nakedness rather than being an advocate for the people. Public nudity is certainly not the norm in society, but is our unwillingness to accept this, due to our British prudish response? If so, then it is in total contrast to a number of countries around the world, some not too far from our own. It is known that before issuing a Visa to live or work in the Netherlands, individuals had to watch a 105-minute film which included gay kissing and topless women on a beach, without objection. While the popularity has fallen, the Japanese are well known for nude public baths, in which the whole family attend. The Spanish, the French and the Italians to name but a few, all seem to be more accepting that there are some members of society who choose the naturist lifestyle. The climate certainly creates an environment for a greater amount of nudity on European beaches, but I don't believe this is the only reason. If it was down to temperature alone then during the summer months there would be no reason for us British not to do the same, but we don't. Perhaps we are unaware that our serious view on many areas of life, also effects how we react to nudity? We are so different in our approach to many things compared to the rest of Europe, for example, working hours, relaxation, drinking. Whether we like it or not, we brits are obsessed by rules, and instead of 'laizzez-faire' and 'c'est la vie', we are completely the opposite. The relaxed lifestyle that welcomes a European siesta and a halt from work in the midday sun, also seems to be the one that is relaxed about topless sunbathing. While this is a way of life in Barcelona, no one could ever imagine a similar scenario in Southend-on-sea, even if it was the same temperature. Our emphasis on proprietary living, seems to prevent a relaxed culture where even bare breasts on a beach are abhorrent. In fact, to be proper in the sense of being British even seems to override the law of the land. As I read the law on nudity, it appears that this act in itself, even in a public place, is not an offence at all. However, and this is the difficult part, a person can be prosecuted if by being nude they cause upset, shock or alarm to others. This is why events such as, 'The Naked Bike Ride' and 'The Mass Skinny Dip' can take place but cycling in a state of arousal will get you arrested. This could also be the case if your neighbour overlooks your garden while you are sunbathing in the nude and they are shocked or alarmed. British law on nudity is in fact is very similar to the rest of Europe although some countries add legal clarity regarding the amount of nudity allowed in a public place. Although the French are more relaxed about such things, it doesn't mean you can stroll around naked just because you are no longer on British soil. Even the countries with the most relaxed attitudes have rules to prevent naked anarchy. For example, in the Netherlands you can be naked in your own garden, the beach and the gym. Public nakedness is allowed, except on public roads, but not if it causes annoyance.

I once met the famous, or perhaps I should

say, infamous Steve Gough at a nude swim event. I didn't need an introduction, as anyone who has read 'H&E' magazine over the last 20 years will have seen his picture. This guy had literally walked the length and breadth of mainland Britain in the nude and because of this, is known as the 'naked rambler'. Although he may not have necessarily set out to challenge the law on nudity, he did just that and was arrested numerous times and attended court on a number of occasions. There is obviously a difference between acting on others concerns and blatantly being naked anywhere that takes your fancy and to hell with the consequences. Naked rambling in itself is no new phenomena; naturist groups have set out across the countryside for years without causing any disturbance. The emphasis, as the law states, is all about modesty when unsuspecting public are on the same path and avoiding shock or alarm. Unfortunately to date, I have no experience of setting out for a walk naked on home soil, except once in my youth when I ran across a field naked in the dark, but I'm not sure that counts. There is little doubt, that it would be an exhilarating experience but to be honest I would be scared stupid of meeting someone. If the extreme version of skydiving is base jumping, then this is what I would call extreme naturism where what people think is tested to its limits and without passing judgement, it's not for me. That being said, I am always positive about the feeling and experience of being nude in the wide-open outdoors. While we may all have stories, about times we have ventured far beyond the bathroom naked, it's taking the next step beyond the back door, where there are so many benefits to be realised. Starting out on this journey, is not an easy thing to do, as there can be a number of hurdles to overcome, internal influences that directly affect you from considering it, and external pressures such as what people will think. In terms of my own internal influences, I dealt with those years ago. I always long to experience the freedom of shedding my clothes, except if it is cold, as then it becomes some kind of endurance event. I know a couple of friends who swim all year round in the Irish Sea, with costumes on I should add. I would never say it to their faces, but they are completely bonkers! There has only been one occasion where I didn't take up the offer of experiencing a naturist event and to this day, I haven't been able to explain why. I went to a leisure centre in Torquay in the summer of 2000 with the purpose of attending a naturist swim event. However, when I got there, although the naturist event was still on, they explained that due to a double booking, they couldn't use the pool but instead had use of the sauna, steam room and health suite. For some reason at that time, I couldn't face a naturist meeting without emersion in water. I guess there was still some self-acceptance going on in terms of being naked around other people in certain situations, and an event with no water at that time was a step too far. It wasn't that I cared about people seeing me naked, or in any way, that I was dealing with how my body appeared to others, it was perhaps the event itself that seemed to obscure.

Generally speaking, Europeans tend to have leaner bodies than their United Kingdom neighbours and this is certainly reflected on the French or Spanish beaches I have visited. So, when visiting any naturist event back home there would tend to be a greater variety of body types, or to be blunt, we tend to be fatter. Most naturists attending a swim seem to be quite happy doing their stuff and so couldn't give two hoots to their appearance. This isn't to say that every naturist is happy with how their own body looks, as body image can cause a great deal of anxiety. While most of us would have a degree of concern when we recognise that we could do with shedding a few pounds, for others this feeling can be crippling. When attending local swimming baths, we have all seen people wearing a tea shirt or shorts over their costumes and without stating the obvious one assumes it makes the person less self-conscious about their appearance. However, after attending a number of naturist swims, the amusing thing is, that some of the most overweight people I have seen in a swimming pool have been naked. Being in this state and having a far from perfect body, one would think that such individuals have every right to be more self-conscious, however this seems not to be the case. Like jumping into a cold plunge pool after a hot sauna and just dealing with the coldness, bearing all very quickly helps you come to terms with how you are perceived. While in no way belittling those who suffer anxieties with their own body image, maybe taking the plunge into naturism would help people see that unlike most of society, naturists are far less obsessed with self-image and tend to be more accepting of differences. I have seen a number of people attending their first ever naturist event, who seem understandably nervous. However, after half an hour of chatting to a number of people, they often appear quite relaxed. What seems initially to be the ultimate test of both self-acceptance and reaction of onlookers, is quite often nothing of the sort. Although for the newbie, there is more than just dealing with their own nakedness, there is the perception of what naturists are? Depending on preconceived ideas, or what you've been told, you could expect a number of outcomes. This could range from expecting to meet a friendly bunch of people, to expecting a group of sexually provocative exhibitionists who spend the whole time looking at each other's genitals. As long as the event is a genuine naturist one, any newbie will either be quickly reassured or if they were expecting something else, be quite disappointed. In fact, there is usually no 'body watching' instead, just lots of friendly chatter, especially when there is someone new on the scene. Nakedness itself is ignored, as it would actually be odd drawing attention to it.

So why in the naturist setting is nudity ignored, when in other scenarios it may be seen as provocative? Is there a difference between nudity and sexual nudity? The answer to this question undoubtedly has everything to do with how the other person reacts. A person enjoying the feeling of wearing no clothes or no swimming costume meeting with others of the same mind will know they share the same understanding of their naked freedom. In other words, naturists meeting even for the first time and even in an unusual setting will usually not react to nudity but are likely to interact socially as they have something in common. In the opposite, non-naturist scenario may I suggest the interactions are something along these lines, as they become more complex depending on whether the person is the onlooker or the subject and if both are aware of each other. The onlooker initially may be shocked at seeing the nakedness and so may look away or choose to keep looking. Whether they have been noticed by the nude or not, the looking quickly turns into voyeurism which now may turn simple nudity into sexual nudity on the part of the onlooker? The next steps depend on the mind as the intent gazing arouses, tempts, and maybe craves a sexual reaction. 'The nude', once realising they have been discovered, can cover up and leave, simply ignore the attention or play along and welcome the prying eyes. In this instance the nude is no longer a figure of innocence but instead, shocking and exciting, having the potential to cause arousal to either party. Recognising how nakedness could cause effect, Bernardino a preacher from Siena, Italy (1427) was noted to have said, 'if one of you women here were to strip naked, how many men and how many women would fall into temptation?'

Throughout periods of history, nudity has been at times celebrated and at others, discouraged. In ancient Greece the male nude was held in esteem as athletic prowess and a figure of moral excellence. During the same period, female nudity was considered a symbol of divinity and procreation although in the art world she remained clothed for many centuries. This all changed in the 4th century A.D. when Praxiteles carved a sculptor of a naked Aphrodite,'Cnidian Aphrodite'. However, by medieval times (500A.D. to 1500A.D.) female nudity was a rarity in 'byzantine art' as it became associated with guilt and shame. This style of art was almost entirely concerned with religious expression, and as the nude form was still associated with pagan culture, it was a rarity. Throughout this period, nudity in art was seen as sinful, as it was found to be in the Garden of Eden after Eve ate from the forbidden tree. In addition, opinions regarding sex and nudity were strongly dictated by the church which meant that procreation was almost, the only reason for such activity. With an emphasis on chastity, sex outside marriage in some cases was punishable by death and public nudity such as bathing was strictly forbidden. In complete contrast, the 15th and 16th century gave rise to the renaissance, where the popularity of the nude was once again realised as it was in Greek and Roman times. This theme was depicted throughout the western art world and even religious works were accepted in this new vain. Notable art works of the era include Albrecht Durer (1504) 'Adam and Eve', Jan Gossaert (c.1530) 'Christ on the Cold Stone', Titan (c.1520) 'Venus Rising from the Sea' and Jean Bourdicha 'Bathsheba Bathing' to name but a few. It was almost as though the nude during this period had reached a 'mythical state' and had become more notable than the art itself. Kenneth Clarks (1956) influential book on the subject, 'The Nude: A Study in Ideal Form' suggested that nakedness was a state in which someone may be embarrassed but 'the nude' was for the educated and had no uncomfortable overtone. Furthermore, he states that 'the nude is not merely the subject of art but a form of art in itself. The nude plays a role similar to that of a hero in an epic: it provides the means and occasion to figure forth what a particular society takes to be the greatest excellence'.

A hidden nude in a seemly repressive 'middle ages' later becomes idealised and held in high esteem during the renaissance, but was this just a reflection of the values, beliefs or even morals of society at the time? Art and literature dating back to ancient Greek and Roman times (600B.C. to 300A.D.) had little in the way of censorship, as much was openly nude and even pornographic in nature. Public nudity in the western world during this period was the norm, so much so, that public baths were purposely built for this leisure activity and in 217A.D. the Roman 'Baths of caracalla' were built to accommodate up to 1600 people at a time. This one Roman bath had 3 furnaces on site with its own designated aqueduct supplying hot, warm and cold water for purposes of swimming and enjoying steam rooms 'au naturale'. Whilst there was a freedom in terms of states of dress, this society of 'anything goes' was synonymous with abuse of every kind. The 'Flavian Amphitheatre' in Rome which later became known as 'The Colosseum' made fighting to the death a spectator sport. During its 100 days of games-inauguration, shockingly 9000 animals were killed, which were there to add to the spectacle of the fighting gladiators. There was openness in terms of sexuality and sexual appetites that would have caused controversy in almost every society since. It accepted as natural, that men would be attracted to youths of either sex, which meant that pederasty was actually condoned, as long as the younger male partner was not a freeborn Roman. From perhaps the most read book of all time, comes a description of this era that sets a graphic scene: 'women exchanged natural relations for unnatural ones; in the same way men also abandoned natural relations with women and were inflamed with lust for one another' (Romans 1 v 26&27. The Bible). The fall of the Roman Empire (300A.D.) in the western world, meant that for around 1000 years there was a lack of rule and organisation, but with 'God's word', the book of rules for living, the church stepped in and led the almost entirely illiterate society. The Roman period of lust and debauchery was seen as sinful and in total contrast to what the new testament of the Bible taught which was written during the same period. As read in the book of Galatians 5 v 19-21: 'The acts of the sinful nature are obvious: sexual immorality, impurity and debauchery, idolatry and witchcraft; hated, discord, jealousy, fits of rage, selfish ambition, dissensions, factions and envy; drunkenness, orgies and the like'. During the 'dark ages' people perhaps conformed more out of fear of punishment than any religious conviction in itself? Instruction came solely from church elders who needed to be educated enough to understand Latin as throughout the middle ages the Bible was not available in English. Nakedness as a subject hardly gets a mention in the Bible accept in the book of Genesis but at no time is this described as a sinful act in itself. It was natural for Adam to have no clothes, so there was no shame. Adam was always naked but never uncomfortable until something made him feel uncomfortable. Ultimately it was the disobeying of God, portrayed in the sin of eating from the tree that made Adam aware of his nakedness and suffered shame for what he had done. Metaphorically, his soul was stripped of native clothing which up until that time, was purity and holiness and therefore following the sin, he could not appear before a pure and holy being.

By the time of the enlightenment during the fourteen hundred's, the church had lost some of its rule over individuals. The now comparatively educated society rediscovered freewill, and with fewer rules and less censorship, folk were free to live how they pleased, but this was a much toned-down version compared with ancient times. Western society had fundamentally changed; while there was freedom on one hand, there now existed an underlying moral code with its roots set in Christian values and laws. Nevertheless, while this was the case, it was noted in Florence during this time that 17000 men were accused of sodomy out of a total population of 40-50000. Diverse sexual practices and freedom to depict art with both male and female nudity meant this was in some respects similar to Greek and Roman times. Nudity in sculpture and paintings was commonplace, but public bathing and exercise in the nude never made its way back into society in the western world after around 400A.D. Although individuals appeared to regain the freedom of choice, the growing influence of Protestantism and Catholicism meant public behaviour was kept in check, especially in the world of art. Alarmingly, statues dating back to the Roman era were defaced, or to be precise, the penises were covered or removed. Pope Clement XIII (1758-1769) had the Vatican produce fig leaves for statues that still sported penises. However, Pope Pius IX (1857) ordered that any statues that included uncovered penises to be totally destroyed. In fact, during this era, many other religious leaders took action and voiced concerns about the depiction of nudity. Michelangelo's painting of the Sistine chapel ceiling faced a degree of censorship by the commissioning Pope Julius II in 1508. However, when he was asked to come back and paint the chapel wall depicting 'The Last Judgement' (1536) Michelangelo insisted on free rein, painting initially over 300 nude figures under the watch of Pope Clement VII. The work took over 4 years and prior to completion Pope Paul III took his place in the Vatican. The differing reforming views may have influenced the fact that many nudes were partially covered by painted draperies before completion.

If we fast forward 500 years or so, we arrive at the early 21st century where in many respects, society has changed very little apart from the fact that nudity is not as openly accepted. For example, apart from seeing works of art in a gallery, it would be unusual to own and display a nude painting or photograph on a wall in our homes. Neither would we prance around the garden while others marvelled at our athletic bodies, as in ancient times. While the naked body is less openly celebrated, on the whole there is an indifference on the subject, where preferring to be nude is reserved more so for the eccentric. Therefore, nudity appears to be seen as neither abhorrent nor overtly censored. There seems to be an unwritten rule in society where individuals have their own private values, morals and beliefs. This means that variations in sexual expression and explicit nudity are commonplace behind closed doors, which to some degree has been the ways things have been for centuries. While sexual deviant behaviour and pornography addiction is hardly ever discussed, our somewhat hypocritical society seems to have limits to what is seen in public with a, 'you can do whatever you like, as long as I don't have to look at it or listen to it' approach. Or to look at this in the context of the subject in hand, 'you can be naked behind closed doors, a designated nude beach or a private club but if you are nude sunbathing in the local park, I am likely to be shocked or offended'.

Having gone full circle, we are back to perception of nakedness, in particular, the British view of it. On the banks of the Isar, in the centre of Munich, it is commonplace and therefore not alarming to see naked bodies sunbathing and swimming. This whole concept is totally alien to the UK, even though the nudity laws for both countries are very similar and so there is little that can be offered in the way of explanation. We see a nude in public and think, rude or illegal. It is as if we think that nudity automatically leads to explicit sexual nudity, or perhaps because it's unclear, this is our fear. In most cases, nakedness and explicit exhibitionism are two separate scenarios completely. However, acceptance of this, even if a person is doing their best to avoid being an exhibitionist, appears to be a step too far. Viewing of nakedness in an art gallery is safe, because once the art has been seen, it can be categorised and deemed as acceptable or not. However, real life nudes spotted on a riverbank having a 'skinny-dip' could be innocently enjoying the freedom of an all over suntan, or they could be sexual exhibitionists. From the onlooker's point of view, the danger is, there is no way of knowing which scenario they have stumbled upon. The poor individual quietly enjoying a nude dip in the river is left wondering how the onlooker has interpreted what they saw, and if they should scarper before the police arrive. There is no getting away from the fact that we do need to chill-out about the subject.

It's Just Not Cricket

If you scan the internet or naturist publications for swim events around the country, and if you read enough of the entry requirements listed, eventually you will come across the phrase, 'only bonafide naturists welcome '. When I first read such a statement many years ago, I was quite taken a back, as if there was a suggestion that you had to in some way prove you were a naturist prior to attending. Also, I asked myself, if you weren't a naturist why would you want to attend a naturist swim? The obvious answer to this, may be to have a good look at the naked bodies, but as already stated, any naturist club, swim event or beach are the most non-sexual environments imaginable, which anyone visiting with the wrong intentions would soon discover. Although the precise definition of what naturism is, may differ for each person, most clubs or events will allow for variations that fit within publicised boundaries. For example, some like to exhibit exotic piercings, some like to show off their all over tattoos, others known as 'smoothies' shave all their body hair except on their head. Oh, I'd better add, that's men and women. In fact, most naturist events or clubs, in order to be recognised themselves as bonafide, will conform to guidelines of a national recognised body which for the UK is 'British Naturism' and for France is the 'Federation Francaise de Naturism'. However, someone new to the idea of enjoying nakedness could easily stumble upon a 'swinging' or 'hedonism' resort, and never discover true naturism with its uncontaminated liberating freedom. While I have no intention of saying that certain groups or clubs promoting nudity are right or wrong, the truth is, some are inherently different to early naturist values as promoted in the post war era. If I use this description of naturism as a guide, then some of the nudity I experienced on my travels was certainly in contrast to this first intended innocence and freedom.

Perhaps the most notorious naturist site in France or perhaps the world, is Cap d'Adge, however the beginnings of this site are in no way representative of what it has become today. In the 1960's the commune of Agde as it was known, consisted of just a few small houses. The area that has now been developed into a naturist metropolis, was first owned by the Oltron brothers. After the second world war, the brothers allowed people to use the land for camping and became aware that people had a preference for swimming and sunbathing in the nude. Over time the camp grew and became popular, especially to young families, and in 1973 the beach was officially designated as 'naturist'. In the early days, the naturist village was a place where voyeurs and exhibitionists were not welcome. Today Cap d'Agde is a large family style naturist resort, or in terms of its size, would be better described as a town. Often referred to as 'naked city', this self-contained place for nudity consists of 2500 camping pitches, apartment complexes, a hotel, shops, restaurants, night clubs, bars, a bank and well over a hundred other businesses. Nudity is legal throughout the whole resort even to the point of sailing into the port and walking off a boat, without a stitch on. As already stated in previous chapters, this resort has a side which at best, means it remains at the extreme side of naturist ethics and at worst, means it is now a hotspot for swingers and libertines. This reputation means that family groups may think twice before a visit. In fact, when researching the site online there was a well-known review company that stated, 'warning, be careful as there is a lot of unsavoury activity that happens in the dunes and on the beach'. The reality is, that this is an unfair description of most of the beach as any adult activities are confined to an area set just off to the edge of the resort itself. However, because such activity occurs both on and off the beach, since 2009 the site is no longer supported by the Federation Francaise de Naturisme. Cap d'Agde is both a naturist resort and a place to for sexual nudity, as a voyeur and a participant. The lines are blurred; there is no separation or partitioning between the two scenarios, anywhere on the site. As a result, true naturism is contaminated as sexual lust and enjoying the feeling of innocence and freedom, don't mix. In many ways, this site seems to mirror the hippie culture of the of the 1960's where nudity and pleasure seeking were synonymous.

The anti-establishment movement first began in the U.K. and spread to the U.S. throughout the 60's and 70's. There were a number of 'counterculture' groups at the time, who campaigned about social issues such as civil rights, human sexuality and women's rights. The 'hippies' as they were known were initially a youth movement comprising of mostly students, which stood for all these things and quickly which developed into a new subculture. This modern 'bohemianism' or 'hippie' lifestyle reflected the mood and trends of the time and became synonymous with experimentation of psychoactive drugs and pleasure seeking. This relaxed view on life meant that public nudity was commonplace; some believing that the 'hippies' were the beginnings of naturism itself, even though this had begun decades before in Europe. This era of nakedness and drug induced dancing culminated in the 1967 'summer of love'. This summer-long event took place in the

Haight-Ashbury district of San Francisco where 100,000 people gathered in hippie dress or in some cases without dress. Although these gatherings happened elsewhere across the U.S. this was the most publicised and became the time when the media reported this as a revolutionary new movement. The group became well known for slogans such as 'make love, not war' and 'flower power'. These were statements of a non-violence ideology, and during this period were quoted during demonstrations against the Vietnam War.

The practice of nudity is well known in a number of subcultures. Perhaps some of the most well-known of these would be hedonism or swinger gatherings and could maybe include the 'burning man festival'. Although the burning man festival doesn't focus on sex, hedonism and swinging are synonymous with nudity and as much sex as possible. From a hedonistic perspective, there certainly would be a great deal of enjoyment to be had, but obviously nudity in this setting is very much about voyeurism and sexual excitement. The beginnings of this type of pleasure pursuit were first noted in Greek philosophy and very much continue in society today. Hedonism as a way of life, is about total devotion to pleasure and happiness to the max. The most extreme form of hedonism is that of the libertines or libertinage, where views on moral and sexual restraint are seen as unnecessary, or even harmful. Obviously not all nudity can be classed as 'naturism', as the philosophy of certain groups and activity of enjoying nakedness, are a world apart. A poignant example of this, was a conversation I had with a local French man while in Cap d'Agde. He had attended the resort for many years and seemed to quite enjoy the opportunity to freely describe some of the things he had seen. Not surprisingly, these tales involved lots of nudity but because of where we were, were not remotely connected to naturism. While the aim of this book is recalling my 'man holiday' exploits, it is about the discovery of naturism not stories of obscenity, so for this reason I choose not to repeat his words. Although I had made a deliberate journey to Cap d'Adge, by the time his mind-boggling tales had come to an end, coupled with the things I's seen, I vowed never to return. Just before we parted company, he said something which acknowledged that Cap d'Adge was very much 'off-track' in terms of naturist values.

"As you say in English, it's just not cricket" While this made me laugh, I really couldn't have put it better myself. In fact, the saying is not English at all, it's very much Australian. It means that something is unjust or just plain wrong, being done to something or someone, but he had used it in the right context, nevertheless.

So, when is naturism not naturism? Given my examples of sex and nudity, the answer appears to be simple, however occasionally the lines are blurred. TV documentary mostly shows a balanced and unbiased view of the subject and because it is for a general audience would actually show little in the way of nudity. On the other hand, there are numerous documentary style naturist videos available that show naturists carrying out certain activities such as horse riding or a pool party, for example. The majority of these films depicting people in the nude, lack any commentary and so completely miss any explanation of the culture or give the audience an insight into the experience. Instead, most film is observational, and some give the impression that the event was only set up to make a film and throw doubt on whether the participants are even naturists. The most concerning and negative aspect of so-called naturist documentary is the focus on the female sex and the fact that there is no lower age limit. As far as I'm concerned, there is little to be gained in viewing naturists on film, as the whole point is to experience the feeling of it. Therefore, I am left with the view that uncensored naturist documentary serves no other purpose than voyeurism, making it totally detrimental to those being filmed and to naturism as a whole. The subject of naturist magazines would not be a dissimilar one. There have been many general naturist publications over the years which toe the line in terms of decency and inclusion of both sexes. 'H&E' would over the years have included some photography but never biased towards one age group or gender and never voyeuristic. It would also include a range of articles featuring general naturist discussion, popular hot topics, holiday destinations and personal experiences. However, throughout Europe there have been a number of pictorial publications over the years which have gone way beyond the lines of decency, some of which I have actually seen for sale at naturist events in the 90's. It seemed in the past, that by making a film or magazine 'naturist' as long as there was nothing explicit on show, there was nothing to stop younger models being featured as well. Although such magazines are now banned, the fact that they existed was yet another sad example of something that was never naturism.

If the assumption is, that all naturists who attend a club, campsite, beach or swim are inherently voyeurs, then there would be agreement that events should be for adults only. Evidence of such activity during any gathering on the whole is absent as the focus is usually on anything but nudity. There would certainly be a number of people in society, usually non-naturists, who believe that it is wrong for younger generations to be naked in such places, as if in some way they will be forever scarred by the experience. It is obvious that any person should be able to make their own choice whether to be naked on a beach or in a pool and this should be no less the case for a youngster. However, in reality, it is usually the adult who has issues with nudity and not the child, as is the case in my family. Lucy Rahim wrote an article for The Telegraph (26/01/2017) about two female naturists who gave their opinions. They suggested that age does not matter and although there is a stereotype of naturism being for just the elderly, it is also for families with young children. They also state that it is a positive community for children which does wonders for self-esteem; it is also a great way to socialise and somewhere that you can be your real self. While saying how relaxing and liberating it was, they also make the point that there is nothing sexy about being naked. When researching nakedness and families on the British Naturism website (BN. org.uk, 1999), they make the point that naturism is in no way harmful or detrimental, in fact quite the opposite.

While naturism has a universal definition, by no means is it universally accepted by all? Naturists may view nakedness as liberating freedom; whereas those from a religious perspective may have the tendency to call it sinful. Religions' view nudity in different ways but to take a general view it would be seen as shameful or degrading. For example, many Arabic speaking countries may have the view that a person should be totally covered when in public at all times. Maybe us crazy Europeans have got it all wrong, as covering up actually makes sense, it reduces the likelihood of skin cancer and prevents lustful thoughts. According to the Bible, nudity would have the implication of sinfulness and especially so in the story of Adam and Eve. However, as with many subjects, it depends a lot on one's interpretation. If we take the Bible in isolation and use it as a moral compass, then in fact being nude is never seen as a sin, even in the case of Adam and Eve - as the sin was disobeying God. The trouble is, no matter what is written, the majority of do-gooders think that public nudity is wrong, so a person from a Christian background going nude may be seen in contradiction to what is expected. I guess the thought of a person leaving church on a Sunday to spend the afternoon naked on a beach would not fit with most church goers. So, is being nude in the presence of others who are also nude, incompatible with Christianity? The Bible gives examples of how people turn away from God and get involved with prostitutes, lust, orgies and the like, however being naked is not necessarily about fulfilling ones' desire for sexual gratification. Society has accepted limits for states of dress, and when on a beach this is certainly apparent. Although it's only when a person goes 'all the way' in terms of undress that this invites comments, and 'the church' may be one institution that would be quick to state it's view on moral grounds. One may be excused for thinking that religion is just about adhering to a set of rules or following a moral code, or perhaps that the view of the church is a definition of right or wrong in society? I believe we all have a duty to conform, to a degree, to what society expects, whether on religious or moral grounds but sometimes I get the impression that being 'good enough' in the eyes of some, is an impossible task. As far as I'm concerned whether naked or clothed, it makes no difference, as the measure of a person's morality is how their eyes or mind lead them astray. The Bible is in fact very clear on this subject and highlights how all men will always be far from perfect, 'Why do you call me good? Jesus answered. No one is good – except God alone.' Mark 10, 18. Also 1 John 1, 8 'If we claim to be without sin, we deceive ourselves and the truth is not in us.' So, if the bible suggests that mankind can never truly take the moral high ground, this makes things simpler, as we are all on a level playing field, but where does this leave nudity? Perhaps naturism is something that a person has to work out for themselves in terms of whether it is right or wrong?

During my second visit to Montalivet, I returned

to my tent one evening to hear some guitar playing and singing, not far away. I listened while as I ate my evening meal, which was more than likely a burger and fries, and then headed over for a closer look. I managed to get the attention of a young lady who spoke English and asked what they were singing and if they were part of an organised group. To my surprise they were a group of young Christians who were staying on the site and obviously had no fundamental issue with naturism, otherwise they wouldn't have been there. Of course, in the evening almost everyone wears clothes but during the day they were as naked as everyone else. If I was honest, until that encounter, I would have waivered on the fence in terms of whether naturism was seen as pure and innocent or bordered on deviant. I never actually felt that naturism was a bad thing but at the same time being a regular church goer, I had uneasiness about telling anyone where I had been on holiday. My naturist activities are still something I don't openly discuss but am always ready to defend, in terms of having nothing to do with sexual deviance in any way. I have since discovered, that there are many Christian naturist groups throughout the UK and Europe alike. According to such groups, nudity is seen as wrong in the following circumstances: when it is forced upon a person, when it is associated with orgies and the like, prostitution, or in the modern-day world, indecent exposure and finally if through suffering, a person has a lack of clothing. When it comes right down to it, religious or not, most would agree that clothing doesn't prevent wrongdoing or sinfulness. Perhaps put a different way, clothed or naked, Adam and Eve would have still displeased God with the eating of the apple and while nudity itself wasn't the wrongdoing, ashamed of what they had done their naked paradise came to an end.

Nudity from the perspective of a naturist may be somewhat different to that of the rest of society, as of course, people are generally more comfortable keeping their clothes on. However, naturists not only want to be naked but are often keen to describe the feeling of it using words like, freedom, relaxation or refreshing, which may differ depending on surroundings. They may also make comments about how it changes their mood or affects their personality in terms of openness or being less self-conscious. Once naturism has been experienced for any length of time, it certainly puts a new perspective on things. For example, I couldn't have ever imagined anything more relaxing than a sauna, steam or Jacuzzi before I discovered naturism on a French beach. In a similar way I always enjoyed the feeling of freedom and being away from it all when walking in the mountains but the first time I shed my clothes in C.H.M. this made me think again. While naturism in this place is my favourite chosen pastime, I recognise that as with any form of pleasure it has its limitations. So, in order to present a balanced view on the subject, I will clearly state what I believe naturism isn't.

In the same way that climbing a mountain will not release you from a fear of heights, naturism will not release you from all your troubles. While there are a number of benefits from being naked in the hot summer sun, one could equally argue that some of those could equally be realised in a sauna. When people talk about effects of nakedness, they often mention the word 'freedom'. While there is undoubtedly a 'feeling' of freedom from the norms that society imposes, ultimately this is no more than a feeling of freedom from clothes. It may give you the 'feeling' of being removed from the worries and pressures of life, but this relative freedom of being nude will not actually set you free. Naturism is also not some kind of spiritual enlightenment, or type of pagan worship where people dance around carrying out naked rituals. However, at the heart of naturist philosophy is the belief that a person can find innocence and purity; in the original state that we were born one is able to free their mind of the restraints imposed by the education of society. I personally believe that while in a large, organised event or resort, nakedness merely shifts to be the new normal and people adapt in terms of behaviour for the time they are present, nothing more. While there is a feeling of innocence because everyone is naked and making no fuss about it, innocence in itself is not something I recognise in naturism. This is not because I believe there to be anything untoward about it, it is more about my own beliefs that in fact no one is truly innocent. As a stereotypical bunch of builders may wolf whistle down the street at a passing young lady, there have been times when I have seen guy's heads turn at a beautiful young lady naked on the beach. I am in no way saying it is wrong to marvel at a beautiful body whether male or female, I am merely stating that naturism doesn't in anyway turn people into saints, they are still human. I have been as candid as I dare while I have recounted my journeys through this subject, but I have deliberately also not included everything. The point is, that while I long to spend a few days every year naked on a French beach, naturism is not some magical remedy that will solve the world's problems, far from it. Finally, I have occasionally used the word 'paradise' in descriptive terms when I refer to that special beach in Montalivet, as if it were some ultimate aim or place where everything was perfect. In hindsight I feel this word is only used as a metaphor for how naturism is set apart from the rest of society, seeking to be different. Instead of being naked on a beach, my own belief is that true paradise can only be found by being in the presence of God, and if this is the case, suggesting anything else seems ridiculous.

On balance, accepting that naturism isn't going to change the world any time soon, I have my preference, and can't wait to be part of the naked throng every year, on that stretch of French beach in Montalivet. Like any subject that isn't well known, it's difficult to put into words. It's always more than just being naked or a naturist, when you are there, it's a cultural thing. C.H.M. is a community with different rules than the rest of society and everyone there, is totally relaxed about it. I don't enjoy the feeling of being there just because of the nakedness; it's far deeper than that, it's a feeling. Although everyone is potentially making themselves completely vulnerable, all hang-ups are cast aside and instead there is a feeling of acceptance and community that ignores body and focuses on the person. Most of us couldn't imagine being naked with our mother or father, however in C.H.M. whole extended family groups, meet together, to enjoy weeks on end in the sun. When I see how happy, how accepting and how natural these people look together, I know that in the same scenario my friends or family would love it. Maybe that was a giant leap too far? Taking friends or family who I have never been naked with, to a naturist resort in France, is perhaps 'pie in the sky'. Most of C.H.M's French, Danish or German inhabitants seem relaxed about such things, but us British often take more convincing. Although I consider myself one of the lucky ones who has slipped through the net, I know given a chance, all my friends and family would enjoy it, just the same as myself. It's an interesting emotion…. in private I imagine that maybe this summer we might visit my paradise together as a family, but I'm too scared to talk about it. I want to tell my best friends and family about the experience, to convince them to give it a try but I have the feeling they'll see me in a new light, and this may be to my detriment. Until I'm brave enough to be open about it, I'll continue to have an internal monologue that goes something along the lines of, 'if you only knew what it was like, if only I could tell you'. Until that day, my winter memories of those summer experiences, will make me feel like the luckiest guy on earth.

Making a statement

I was just about to jump in the shower before setting off for work, when I remembered I had left a new can of shaving gel in the kitchen. To avoid making the floor wet, I decided to pop down the hall and collect it before I began. As I've said before, I don't make a habit of walking around the house naked but surprisingly the response I received from my wife and kids was not what I expected. Ignoring my nakedness in the wrong part of the house, common sense took over as they enquired, 'aren't you freezing cold?' Although the south west coast of France tends to be warm during the summer, it's not always 30-degree heat, all of the time and whether during the day or evening, there are times when you just have to cover up to keep warm. Nudity is something to be enjoyed, not a fool hardy endurance event whatever the weather. Although I can remember one occasion during a rainy afternoon, when having only been on the site for a few hours I decided I was going nude and to hell with appearances. I stupidly strolled around in the rain wearing just a pair of sandals and a silly smile on my face. The inner contentment and the feeling of freedom I had sought, meant the chill of the rain wasn't standing in the way of my much-awaited experience. I received a number of odd glares which I'm sure wasn't just the lack of protection against the elements, more the stupid grin on my pale-skinned face. To any regular resident, I was one of the newbie tourists, which can be very easy to spot with a pale white or burned pink complexion.

As mankind has adapted and survived the elements, he has obviously used plants or animal skins prior to the jump to cotton, silk or nylon. In fact, historians suspect that human survival rates improved only after they began to wear clothes some 83000 to 170000 years ago. After stumbling upon this bit of historical guesswork, the thought did cross my mind that this must have been one of the least taxing theories ever dreamt up. It's not rocket science; the human body gets too hot or too cold and you're dead in no time at all. Outdoor naturism is a lovely idea for a lucky few around the world and for everyone else its pie in the sky, maybe only reserved for the Garden of Eden story in a book.

Of course, clothes are not just about self-preservation, there are occasions, even in a naturist resort, where certain people are always dressed. When you first arrive at C.H.M. reception you are not instantly greeted by nudity, as to be honest that would be weird as everyone would require a pierced nipple to hang their name badge from. Instead, there are smartly dressed reception staff in matching uniforms, name badge, a smile and a 'hello can I help you?' to go with it. The reception building, the counter, the uniform, the friendly staff are all part of the package to check you in to the experience. It says to anyone who arrives, 'you are checked in, accepted and this is where your experience begins'. In a similar way, security staff usually walk or drive around the site in a dark grey uniform with walkie-talkie at the ready, doing whatever security guards do. The car with the flashing lights and 'security' written down the side, the uniform, the radios, all make a statement, 'we are here for your safety, to check everything as it should be'. The lifeguards wear matching red t-shirts and go about their 'watching no one is drowning' routine, but they are more relaxed. Although a lifeguard is probably the most important of all jobs, I said relaxed. I make this mis-judged statement for one reason alone; they only wear the t-shirt and nothing else. There is nothing at all to suggest they don't take their job seriously or are less caring in how they go about their task, but the lack of uniform without meaning to, makes a statement. On the plus side, the 'half uniform' helps them come across as more approachable and just the same as everyone else, which is no bad thing. I must add that lifeguards can also be seen with shorts and a coat when required but full uniform, appears not to be mandatory. The only remaining uniform I'm aware of is that of the staff in the resort shop, the 'Spar'. Wherever you enter a spar anywhere across Europe, the uniform is the same, even in C.H.M. While lifeguards spend the day looking at naked bodies, you would think that they would be the ones who would look twice. However, the only time I've ever seen that kind of reaction is from the staff in the Spar. In a strange way, it is one of the only places on the site that is trying to be like the outside world apart from its clientele.

Many sports can be carried out in the nude but when contact or safety requires it, an extra layer is added. Being a beach resort, C.H.M. lends itself to water sports and is synonymous with surfing in particular. There is no hard and fast rule that a wet suit is required but anyone who has tried surfing in anything but calm waters, will have found that sand, saltwater and a board can also be a painful abrasive against the skin. There is also the fact that the sea even on the warmest of days can leave you verging on exposure without at least a 6mm wetsuit. Simply wearing a wetsuit makes a statement; on one hand it makes you part of the surfing crowd, whether for fun or a serious surfer, secondly it makes you feel like a surfer. Wear a suit and casually amble around any supermarket or department store, and sooner or later someone will approach and ask you where something is, as if you are a member of staff. A foreman walks onto a building site, in bright protective clothing holding a clip board and the rest of the staff will take notice or even change what they are doing. The fact is, what you wear changes perceptions of those around you and even yourself. A policeman or woman doesn't become an officer of the law by merely being successful in an interview or completing the required training. It's not until the institutionally recognisable uniform is worn, does the individual truly feel they have become an officer. A uniform is such a powerful symbol that not only the person wearing it but everyone who sees it, starts to act differently. I can remember in my late teens almost breaking out into a sweat every time I saw the police uniform or still worse the uniform and the car together. As a paranoid teenager, it wasn't necessarily that I was up to no good, it was that I may look like I was up to no good. Although uniforms are merely clothes, there effects are varied and far reaching. Some costumes, outfits or uniforms make us laugh, some command respect and others may cause attraction. Attempting to watch a Morris dancer without a smile on your face would prove difficult but smiling when faced with an armed soldier may not be sensible. Some uniforms have a double effect, for example a fireman is a lifesaver but may also cause ladies to go weak at the knees. The strange thing is, that the same guy in jeans and a t-shirt may be less attractive? Stereotypically, men of course have similar attractions to uniforms, at this point I perhaps shouldn't mention the Britney Spears hit, 'Baby, one more time'. Laws or regulations mean that for certain professions, wearing the wrong clothes can actually be an offence; a police officer on duty out of uniform could be in bother. Equally a member of the public impersonating an officer would certainly be arrested. Some retail organisations have moved away from formal wear to appear relaxed and more approachable, but this can make finding a member of staff troublesome. The retail company I work for recently decided upon a similar theme, stating that as long as the company t-shirt was worn, any other clothes combinations were acceptable. I instantly felt unprofessional and began to explain to customers that it was a non-uniform day. In fact, I felt it was so detrimental to the perception of professionalism, that I rebelled and reverted back to my suit. Once the suit was back on, I felt I was once again the member of staff the public expected and to be without it, was in some way relaxing standards. However, on occasion, the symbol of the manager in the suit is not always welcome, as I found every day, I returned home to a building site. I employed a bricklayer to do the brickwork for me on a kitchen extension, but soon became aware that it wasn't until the suit was replaced by jeans and t-shirt, did he ever talk to me. If I was honest, the suit made me feel a little awkward and once it was out of the way, I felt more relaxed. There is no getting away from the fact, that certain clothes set people apart and cause barriers. Admittedly it's not just the clothes, it's the social position that's assumed from what is being worn, or put another way, its how society values the symbol of the uniform. Whether in a subculture or wider society, what is worn dictates cultural standing or position. I always remember the Leonardo DiCaprio film, 'catch me if you can' when he forged the qualifications and relied on his uniform to let him pass as a pilot, a doctor and a lawyer. There's one line from the film that has stuck in my mind because there's so much truth in it, 'they can't keep their eyes off the pinstripes'. In other words, if you look the part and say the right things, in most cases you can pass as the genuine article. Taking this a step further, there are many who deliberately use clothes in a literal vain attempt to influence their own social position or acceptance. People who pay attention to status and how they are perceived will often buy into the whole package, the car, the house, the job and the designer girlfriend to go with it. Although such a person may appear rich in material possessions,

I have always considered any such existence to be superficial and empty. To my mind, the route to unhappiness is found in comparing possessions with those around you, and this type of existence is something I will never aspire to. Although I am no saint, far from it, I strive to treat everyone the same, no matter who they are and how they're perceived. Perhaps it's just an age thing, whether intuition or a sense of what really matters, as you get older it's easier to see the real person in front of you and discount personal effects. Some of the richest, influential and deep-thinking individuals I have met, care nothing of appearances and instead let their personality and 'real self' do the talking. In this way, confidence comes not from how you think you are perceived, but instead from an inner contentment, not caring what people think. My personal example of this is during the pick-up at the local school and is something which many parents can relate to. As the school has a good reputation, it attracts a fairy affluent crowd, this means many of the mums turn up in cars that could only be described as status symbols. I on the other hand had great pleasure in owning an old and battered VW Golf, which was by far the worst in the car park. I used to laugh at the daily routine of what appeared to be the 'expensive four-wheel drive club' as they all parked together in a line for a chat, coffee in hand. I knew for a fact that if I won the lottery and bought myself a 90k Land Rover, I could easily join them. I always thought that whether a brand-new Land Rover or beaten-up Golf, the person was more important than any branding and I would never be drawn into such a superficial game. So why the focus on clothes, when I should be discussing experiences of nakedness? The fact is, clothes can cause barriers, as people often form an opinion on what they see, before any conversation begins, very much like the school car park.

To say that there is no evidence of social hierarchy in a nudist resort would not be accurate, as every camping pitch or fixed address is different. Some homes are modest, somewhat dated, wooden shacks, while others are state of the art modern houses, and although the emphasis is on simple living, each one of these has a car parked next to it. Although the barriers of clothes are removed, in their own way these four wheeled accessories parked next to each dwelling, make statements about net worth with registration plates, showing the language each person speaks. Its simple human nature to avoid interaction with someone who you think doesn't speak your language, or perhaps is of a different social class. One year I tried out the health suite as it was a particularly cool day and I just fancied the heat of a sauna. While sitting in the steam room I chatted to another guy stating, 'how this may be the warmest we get all day'. It turned out that the man was a French government official who spoke very good English, he went on to explain how he had been onsite for some weeks and was waiting for his wife to finish work to join him. If I had walked past the same guy outside of his accommodation with an expensive French car parked out front, I would have avoided conversation. However, we actually chatted for around half an hour and because there were no barriers to conversation and no preconceptions, we were just two naked guys in the steam room. This is absolutely the same on the beach, walking around the site or swimming in one of the pools, everyone is equal in every sense. It's not until you interact with someone, do you find out who they are.

Whether on the beach or attending one of the pools, the dress code is nakedness. There are signs dotted around the site stating that the site is a clothes free zone, and because of this you would almost expect the security team to go around asking people to disrobe in an attempt to root out any imposters, but fortunately they don't as this would be somewhat worrisome. The only place I've ever seen nudity strictly enforced was when someone tried to swim in the pool wearing a costume. While nudity isn't compulsory, it is what C.H.M. is all about and to be honest if you chose not to conform on the beach or around the pool you would feel very out of place. Although, it's not nakedness all of the time, as for different areas of the site and different times of the day, being clothed appears to be acceptable. When I say clothed, this is quite often only a part covering, for example wearing an item to protect from the sun in the form of a t-shirt or a material wrap often worn by ladies. However, there are times when people wear just shorts, skirts or bikini bottoms which obviously are nothing to do with protection against the elements but more about covering of modesty. To a naturist, the rest of the population who wear clothes are known as 'textiles'. This word literally comes from what clothes are, and clearly sets apart, one group from another. Although in a naturist setting, this word is being used more and more to describe those who seem to have no reason to cover up apart from modesty itself. For the most part, nudity is not expected at 8 o'clock in the morning or indeed at the same time in the evening, but in the heat of the day when wandering around the site, wearing clothes especially just to cover modesty is against the spirit of the place. Naturism is about letting it all hang out, without a care, enjoying the liberating freedom, whatever your age or body condition. The decision to cover one's nether regions in a naturist site makes no sense at all and perhaps one should ask if such a person is really enjoying the experience? However, it is also important to understand that for some there may be a fine line between enjoyment and feeling totally vulnerable. As suggested previously, we are all on a journey in terms of letting it all go and losing our inhibitions and some may find easier than others. As naturists expect the rest of society to relax about nudity, perhaps they also need to be understanding about those who choose not to be naked all of the time? Does this mean that naturists should welcome textiles to sit amongst them on naturist beaches? There is no getting away from it, one experience is much different to the other, and either group are always going to feel uncomfortable on a naturist beach together. The naturists in particular, feeling as if they are being watched by onlookers with unknown motivations. To my mind, mixing things up is a bad idea, especially on a beach, you are either one or another.

If clothes can make a statement, then I believe nudity and naturism makes a stronger one. What I find attractive is the complete lack of ambiguity; a birthday suit can either be worn as male or female, of course making cross dressing in the heat of the day impossible. No one has any agenda in terms of socially trying to outdo the other, as everyone on the beach in a material sense is equal. In fact, if there is any emphasis between naturists at all, it is that of simple living and enjoying every moment. This simplicity is far more than being nude, it's in many ways about leaving normality at the gate as you enter the resort. Believe it or not, in this age of mobile phones and being constantly socially connected, you rarely see a person obliviously staring at a screen. Vast as the site is, one would expect cars to be driving up and down to the beach or the shops but instead there are hundreds of people on foot or bicycles. Being at one with nature and protecting the environment is at the core of the naturist lifestyle. There isn't even a need to worry about what you'll wear the next day, apart from rinsing out the odd t-shirt. There is pretty much no washing required, making things extremely eco-friendly. You only need spend a few days on site, to understand that things run at a much slower pace than the rest of the world. In many ways this is the same as any holiday but with naturism it seems different. Every holiday I have ever had, has been jam packed, without chance to laze around; filled with excursions to the nearest towns or beaches, but on this site, just experiencing the tranquillity, the beauty, the magic and the innocence of being naked, is enough.

As the day changes from afternoon to evening, the crowds ceremoniously move away from the beach and pools. This ushers in a change of atmosphere across the whole site, apart from the frenzy to find a place in one of the many showers. People gradually return to their base camp and get ready for the evening, where they'll usually do one of two things. Either this is a time for home cooking and sitting round with family and friends chatting, or it's a pit stop to maybe put something on before heading out for the evening. As it's a little cooler, people tend to wear something, but you would rarely see anyone put on their best shirt or summer dress, it's just not that kind of place. Instead, people would either fully dress casually, or partly dress in a wrap or t-shirt. Although I've never seen anyone deliberatively dress provocatively in C.H.M, sometimes it can appear a little odd to see a man or woman nude in a crowd of people who are dressed. You get used to 'dressed' and then, all of a sudden, nakedness seems a little out of place, but no one looks twice as it is in no way rude. Imagine heading out to a restaurant in the evening, sitting down to a meal and while everyone is fully dressed, a naked lady strolls in. In normal society, people would stop and stare, but during the evening in a naturist resort, the clientele can dress as they please. I remember an experience at the beach restaurant / bar back in 1996 at around 11.00pm. There was a small dance floor lit by a stack of coloured lights in front of the D.J. and during the warm summers evening, a handful of merry makers were grooving to some tunes. While everyone was dressed in something, one young lady stood out on the dance floor as she just wore a very see-through cotton top. Although she was mostly covered up, one could easily see that she was wearing nothing else. On this occasion, the in-between state was quite appealing to the senses, and remember it as one of the rare occasions in C.H.M. when nudity bordered on becoming a sexual experience. I would certainly say that the item of clothing made the scenario sexier than nudity alone. So, was this just me, or do others sometimes find clothing sexier than no clothes? If I was pushed to answer such a question, I think my answer would be this, and I would reiterate, it all depends on the circumstances. A beach full of nudes is not a turn on but a nude in the bedroom is. A fully clothed person may be attractive and admirable but rarely a sexual turn-on. However, I find that the suggestion of nudity, a short skirt, tight leggings, stockings and suspenders or revealing lingerie, does it every time. The fact is, we are all different in terms of what we find sexually attractive but who would have thought that being on a naturist beach would not turn the average man into a voyeur. If the norm of your surroundings is that nudity is a non-erotic event, then you assimilate, but Cap d'Agde suggests that nudity can also be quite the opposite. If I were to make a statement based on myself and the handful of people I have asked, then I would suggest that most of us find semi-nudity the biggest turn-on. Perhaps I should also base this statement on one other fact, lingerie sales are worth billions every year and between consenting adults, is probably the most popular item of clothing bought as a gift.

It may sound, in the case of clothes verses nudity, I would advocate that we all put the law aside and do whatever we please, but I'm not about to do that. A reckless naked social anarchy would be a confusing world to live in. If nakedness wasn't clearly defined, we would be back to wondering whether the nude before us, has sexual intensions, as previously discussed. I am merely pointing out that given the right circumstances, being without clothes has its benefits. Of course, in day-to-day life, the opportunity to enjoy even a few minutes in the buff is seriously restricted. So, unless you have a secluded garden, a warm conservatory or live in the wilderness, you have little choice but to attend a designated area. Once you've found *your place* to be without clothes, in order to aid the decision on whether to go nude or not, maybe apply some simple but obvious rules. If it's cold, wear clothes, if the sun is too hot wear a hat, sun cream and maybe a t-shirt. If the temperature allows, then wear nothing at all, but to really enjoy the experience you have to find a special place, even if it's only behind the hedge, out of sight of the neighbours. Take note, if your chosen place conflicts with society's codes and laws, find somewhere it doesn't. Be alone if you want to, go with someone else if you prefer. Stay in the U.K. and attend a club, a swim event or find a secret place where you'll never be discovered. Maybe go on an adventure, across the sea to warmer climates, to a European resort or beach. If you are lucky, you'll discover your own paradise, your secret place, never to be forgotten. Whatever you do, wherever you go, very quickly you'll get over the 'nudity' bit and realise that being 'clothes free' can be such a release, maybe even a new beginning?

A Day in the Life

After a day at the office, I came home and spoke to my builder, who explained to me in great detail how he'd battled against the elements trying to lay brick that day. In fact, it sounded like an impossible task, building the two-story gable end, high above the ground, on swaying scaffolding, while open to the elements. I had the impression of it being far more than a physical task, as he described the water running down his neck and how the cement trowel blew off the wall to the ground below. He said that he'd considered taking some photos or even a video to capture the experience but decided that this wouldn't adequately convey the working environment, or how he'd felt. In the same way, seeing photos or even videos of the site in Montalivet, in no way captures or tells the story of the actual experience. Therefore, my task is clear, to capture the senses and emotions of the reader as I tell the story of a day in Centre Helio Marin.

Although I have a fondness for sleeping in a tent, without doubt it provides the least protection and so a day can start a lot earlier than expected. The nylon walls provide almost no barrier to the chatter of passers-by or distant entertainment, and when the rain falls you can't even hear yourself think. Whenever I go on one of my 'man holidays', I pack so light that I have to make do with the minimum of mattress's, as a result I never wake feeling bright and breezy, ready for the day ahead. Even thoughts of the thin mattress, remind me of the pain I suffered from my ribs as I woke. My nights in C.H.M. were always the same, in terms of being in-touch with the environment and feeling close to nature. Any external noise or extreme of weather was never an unwelcome distraction, as this was the beating heart of the site and I wanted to sample every hour of it. It was always the same every morning as I fought to get back to sleep, the pain of the uncomfortable sleeping position, coupled with the heat of the morning sun shining through the material of the tent keeping me awake. Even if I opened the zipped door for cooler air or shuffled to find a more comfortable position, it never made any difference…. getting back to sleep was impossible. Through the drowsy state, the morning sounds of the campsite quickly bring you to a reality of where you are, not at home in your comfortable bed but instead somewhere far superior. The sounds of the pine trees overhead swaying in the coastal breeze and the clattering of bicycles setting out across camp are the best alarm clock ever. I never remembered sleeping much past 8 o'clock but the sounds in the air make it clear that people are already awake and going about their daily activities.

A memory

As I venture out of the tent, finding my sandals where I'd left them the night before, I see the toilet block in my sights and head in that general direction. There are many seasoned campers onsite who bring their own bicycles, each one with its own carrying rack. As I walk along the stony path towards the loo, people cycle past in various state of undress carrying different combinations of loads, some with towels and washing accoutrements, others with goods from the on-site shops featuring the obligatory French loaf. As I walk back from the loo towards the tent, I decide what to do with the morning while at the same time wishing I had been more awake before I'd had set off. I unzip the tent and do my best to think ahead trying to avoid meaningless journeys backwards and forwards, while at the same time trying not to carry too much. I pack my small rucksack with some money, shampoo, toothbrush, a razor and an apple left over from the day before. Knowing I'm better prepared, I set out, purposefully this time, toward a busy shower block near to the central shopping area.

As I enter the shower block, it is busy with the kind of people who like to get up early and do that kind of thing, which is almost entirely the elderly. People politely greet each other with a, "bonjour" but I'm convinced that it's purely a social acknowledgement more than the fact that anyone knows anyone else. I head for the showers and find a quiet corner. I had only brought a t-shirt and sandals' so getting disrobed was no big affair. While the open-air, showers tend to be a little cooler, on the whole the site's indoor showers are not only reliable, but they are also pleasingly hot. I use my shampoo as I always do, wash hair first then everything else with the lather before rinsing. Next, I walk towards the mirrors with the shampoo bottle and grab a toothbrush and razor from the bag on the way. I've packed so light, that I have no shaving gel or toothpaste but manage a shave and brushing my teeth with the shampoo alone, and a lot of mouth rinsing afterwards, yuck! I deliberately didn't bring a towel to keep the weight down on my morning's travels and so after getting my bag together, I step into my comfortable sandals, exit the shower block and air-dry along the short walk to the shops.

Although its nowhere near the full heat of the day, by the time I get to the on-site spar, I'm not only dry but have decided that I really need to buy a bottle of water for the day ahead. I always chose the spar, as my needs were simple and shopping list uncomplicated: fruit, bread, some ham or cheese and a bottle of water. If it wasn't so hot, I would have liked to carry some bars of chocolate as a treat but it always was and so I didn't. Of course, the shopping area caters for far more adventurous palates, there is a shop for each type of food. If I had been lazy, I could have had a sit-down breakfast, but such *luxuries* were not for me today, I left the spar and briefly organised everything into my rucksack, before setting off for a naked walkabout. I exited the commercial area from the opposite side than I had entered, towards the recreation grounds.

As I'm not actually heading anywhere in particular, I walk slowly and breathe in the atmosphere around me. Whenever you stop to take in your surroundings in C.H.M. it's certainly not the nudity that strikes you first, it's the fact that the whole site is set amongst pine trees. The aroma of pine is so thick in the air that you can almost taste it as you breathe in, coupled with the fact that everywhere you go, there seems to be a carpet of pine needles on the ground. These giants in the sky, are welcome shade throughout the day and constantly remind you of their presence with a background noise overhead, as the sea breeze moves through the branches. As the trees waved 'good morning' in the sky, I walked through the last row of mobile homes, away from the residential area, away from the trees and towards the sports grounds. The white noise of branches in the breeze lessens, and the pines release their grip on my senses; it's only now that other background noises become apparent. To keep the shops and restaurants functioning, there's a constant stream of vehicles either delivering goods or occasionally emptying recycling bins. The noise from the bottle bank recycling lorry is unmistakable, especially early in the morning. The drivers of these vehicles are either common visitors or it's a reflection of how relaxed the French are. Although there are naked people wandering around, the drivers appear to be completely uninterested; surely if this was back on UK soil they would act differently? I'm now at the recreation fields which are impressively large for a holiday resort. As I'm not at a natural entrance to them, I can either walk through the middle of the adventure playground, make a detour back towards the site's main entrance or turn right and pick my way between the tennis courts. I chose the latter, as after the tennis courts there was some welcome shade in a covered area with three ping pong tables. An athletic looking German couple were in the middle of what looked to be a very serious game. Keeping out of the sun, I watched them for a while, ate an apple and guzzled down some liquid refreshment. They finished their game and began packing their equipment into a rucksack. I watched them walk away and as my head turned, caught a glimpse of a man lying naked on a table in the building opposite. I threw my apple core in a nearby bin and decided to investigate. As I neared the open door of the building, I could see a group of people in the serious business of drawing while the man laid still. There were a number of artists of mixed ages, taking their time, contemplating their next use of the charcoal on paper. They didn't seem to mind an audience, but I chose not to disturb and deliberately, silently, exited their space. There are several buildings in the recreation area, each one providing activities for the naked residents. The next one I came across was hexagonal in shape, with the doors and windows wide open. when close enough to see inside, I noticed three ladies laid out on yoga mats, moving in extreme slow motion. Once again, this group were better off not being disturbed and I shuffled away as quietly as I'd approached, to see what lay in store around the next corner. I was a little surprised to find that the next building, was a fairly large library. I was greeted by two elderly ladies at a reception area as I walked in, who very politely asked if I needed any assistance. As I couldn't read a word in French, the only thing I could understand were pictures. There were a number of photographic essays showing the history of C.H.M. that were very interesting, something certainly not to be found in any other library. Realising that the morning had now almost become lunchtime, I left the building to notice an empty skateboard park opposite. I decided to leave the recreation area and wander towards the indoor pool but as I left, made a mental note of all the other activities on offer: basketball, football, indoor and outdoor kids club, crazy golf and a number of inflatable bouncy thingies. I thought for a moment that perhaps I would return one day with my wife and kids, although this of course is very unlikely.

As I walk towards the covered pool this takes me past the other side of the shopping area where a que of naked residents, wait in line for the A.T.M. There is now no hint of the stony path, as I follow the smooth tarmac road over some speed ramps through a tunnel of overhanging pine trees. This area has a different feel about it, as it is well away from the camping pitches and is zoned into small residential villages. There are no mobile homes but instead purpose-built wooden houses, each with its own garden. As I walked along, I can just make out the shapes of people through some of the perimeter hedges and distant conversation, but it was difficult to hear anything through the noise of the crickets. The sun had now brought the site up a few degrees, which had two effects, the smell of the pine sap had become even more intense, and the crickets had in some places gone from the odd chirp to a deafening crescendo! As I approached the pool, the health suite with sauna, steam room and Jacuzzi were set back to the right of the road. Unless it was a cold and rainy day, I personally didn't know why anyone would want to attend such a place. The pool has few nearby trees, so as I begin to approach, I can feel direct sun on my head back and face. Nakedness means you get to feel any environmental change instantly, the refreshing breeze, the coolness from the shadows and the heat from the sun, it's a wonderful feeling. Before entering the pool gates, I must follow the code of ceremonially removing any footwear and leave my sandals on the wooden stands provided. The next step is to enter the pool perimeter through the large metal gates which on first attempt seemed to be locked, but discovered after some frustration, only open one way. Once through the gates, total nudity is enforced as you pass through a rise-off shower, obviously there for hygiene reasons, then I'm in. I quickly find a spot for my bag and navigate my way through to the poolside. It wasn't the busiest time of the day for the pool but even so, there were enough people to make it difficult to find a spot to jump in. As I do, I have a slight shock as I'm reminded that the shallow end is on the far side and I've just jumped into the 6-foot end and disappear under the water. With the quick all over change of temperature, I attempt to swim in a straight-ish line to the opposite end but find that there are too many kids in the way to make it possible. Luckily there were two roped off lanes for anyone who preferred to swim rather than just mess around and I adjusted course accordingly. Although I really enjoy swimming, to be honest, it's the feeling of being in the water more than the exercise I love. I stay in for maybe ten lengths before heading for the showers, then off to be reunited with my sandals outside. I feel a new, all-over sensation, as a warm breeze quickly takes me from dripping wet to bone dry as I walk away. Each time a new sensation is felt, I'm reminded that I'm naked and reminded of where I am, this combination makes walking along without a smile, impossible. I'm now feeling hungry and have a spring in my step as I decide to head back to my tent to get supplies before setting off for the beach. Ever since my first visit back in 1994 I've never needed to check the site map. That first year, I remember exploring every corner of the place in detail. Even though I know exactly where I'm going, I like to vary my route or deliberately take the wrong route to add to the adventure. While setting off in the wrong direction, the lack of shade from the trees now reminds me to apply some sun cream, but after hunting through my bag discover there is none. My relaxing walk now changes pace and direction as I realise, I'm quickly turning into a lobster.

I arrive back at base camp and find that I'm not only feeling very warm but am hungry too. Sitting down on ceremony in front of my tiny tent, I rip apart the French stick and stuff in some ham. With a sigh of relief, I devour it along with a bottle of water in double time, and then reach into the tent for my towel which I lay out on the pine-needle covered ground. As I lay down sprawled on the ground, the heat and tiredness simultaneously overwhelm me. For a few minutes I watch the canopy of shade overhead as it moves in the breeze, and then I close my eyes. The subject of any dream was already chosen; I didn't need to dream of anywhere else apart from the place I was in. I drifted off....... Some minutes later I became aware of something crawling over my upper leg. I went from dozing, to fully alert, in a second to find a bloody great wood ant! A big black thing, the size of an adult thumb nail! That put an end to any rest in front of the tent and I quickly decided the beach would be a better place to chill. I made sure I took the sun cream and towel, ditched the food but took the water and set off wearing a t-shirt. I paid particular attention to bringing a towel, as only the day before I had forgotten it and ended up with a rather unfortunate incident. Instead of a towel, I had laid out my t-shirt on the sand to sit on. It wasn't till I stood later that day, to order burger and chips did I notice I was sporting two brown 'skid marks' down the front of the same t-shirt I had sat on. I was so embarrassed; I literally ran back to my tent to get changed. Luckily, I don't think anyone noticed. Slapping some sun cream on my face, neck and arms to prevent any further burning, I set off through the trees and out into the open sun. As I walked past the bicycle racks towards the beach, I was conscious that I was not acting like a hard-core naturist. Everyone else was naked by this point, but because of the intense heat I had a t-shirt and a towel covering my head, leaving just my backside and legs showing. When I finally stepped off the boardwalk onto the sand, my prime concern was getting a good covering of suntan lotion. I stopped at the first clear patch of busy beach, threw everything off, including sandals and covered every bit of skin in as much cream as possible. This was another one of those moments when nakedness instantly senses a change of environment from the heat of the sun and then the cooling sensation from the lotion. It's very difficult to explain, but the first time each day you remove your sandals on the beach while completely naked, it kind of makes you feel as if you've reverted back to your youth. It would have been silly to run around shouting 'Yippee!', but that's exactly how I felt. Is this why I've never seen a grumpy person naked on a beach before?

Thinking about it, every time I went to that beach, I only did one of three things: sit for a while, walk for a while, swim for a while, and then repeat. This was my routine, over and over again, until the crowds drifted back to camp at around 7pm, and then after a while, I left too. The whole camp seems to revolve around routines. The morning is all about washing, shopping, clubs, and other activities. Then usually well after midday, comes lunchtime, which much later than back home, seems to often include a time of relaxation with the family. It's not until 2 or even 3pm that the crowds begin to head for the beach. If it's a hot afternoon, the whole site completely empties onto the beach and the sand colour changes from golden, to bare backside white. By 7pm the lifeguards leave the beach which seems to signal for the majority, the end of the beach session. Although initially the fun pool quickly fills, the time leading up to 9pm is first a rush for the showers, then a combination of eating out and cooking in. Then, some will stay out for evening entertainment, restaurants, or bars, while others sit around chatting in family groups until it's time to sleep. This is the way things go on, some doing their own thing, while others follow the crowds, but whether young or old everyone has the same thing in common, enjoying the feeling and freedom of nudity.

I'll ever forget my visits to Centre Helio Marin. Memories of the early visits may be fading but the way the experience has affected me, it will remain with me for as long as I live. I always make a point of taking home special mementoes and have shells, pine needles and even Montilavet sand which I keep in a secret place in my garage. I have old campsite maps and brochures and some years have even sent away for additional samples to add to my collection. This may sound like it borders on the obsessive, perhaps it does, but I don't care.

While I have a fondness for C.H.M, I am very much a realist. There are some things that this world-renowned site does very well, and some things it could do better. The most positive aspect is undoubtedly the palpable atmosphere, apparent throughout the whole site; this is the making of the place and without this, it wouldn't be the same. An atmosphere is a feeling, I guess while difficult to put into words, in this place has everything to do with the freedom the residents enjoy and experience together, completely unhindered. The facilities take a close second place, the showers, toilets, pools and health suite are all very high quality indeed. Even back in 1994, they may have been old, but they were very impressive. For me, the lifeguards are very much worth a mention as they seem to miss nothing in the pools or on the beach, making you feel very safe in the water. I have a mixed view of the camp's staff except to say that the guys in reception are very welcoming and helpful. At this point it feels as if there is going to be a, 'but if it wasn't for….', but there isn't. There is nothing overwhelmingly negative that would affect your stay, as the feeling of belonging to something uniquely special takes president over everything else. However, if I were to be critical, I would say this special feeling, this amazing atmosphere, perhaps comes more from the occupants than from the site itself. I've already said that welcome is second to none: friendly, efficient, making sure you know where you are going, it couldn't be better. Although after receiving the red-carpet treatment, you seem to be left on your own. I'm speaking entirely from the perspective of a client with a tent and a pitch to find. On every occasion my pitch was either difficult to find or very substandard in terms of it being a usable space. Surely there is little point marking a pitch on a map, or even showing someone to a space, that is impossible to use. If a pitch is just a little uneven or a little too sandy, this is an acceptable inconvenience, but completely overgrown or a pitch with an incline that makes sleeping impossible, is probably not great. While the welcome made you feel great, if you end up with a pitch like this, one would be justified in feeling a little unhappy. There is absolutely no reason why the impressive experience in reception shouldn't carry forward to the experience of a camping pitch. It's not as if C.H.M. site lacks staff, because it really doesn't, nevertheless some areas lack the attention they should be getting. Most major holiday companies or resorts pride themselves in being totally customer experience focussed, and often actively pursue customer feedback. The fact is, most of us don't demand excellence, and there is probably a middle ground where most are happy. Although this may seem a little idealistic or unreasonable on my part, I do feel that if the staff in C.H.M. were a little more approachable or made an effort to actively interact and enquire if everything was satisfactory, it may make all the difference. The fact is, this is one person's subjective and very critical opinion and as the site is next to perfect in so many respects, maybe also a little unfair.

Before booking a holiday most of us will check reviews, in an effort to get a real and balanced view and then when you visit you can form your own opinion. If a holiday company cares about reputation and ultimately visitor numbers, then customer reviews should be important. However, C.H.M. is different, it's not a normal holiday resort, and it offers something completely different. Both naturism and its iconic status set it apart, not only from normal holiday resorts but from other naturist venues in France. Although Centre Helio Marin will always have a steady stream of naked customers, instead of merely operating as a business, I believe this 'world's first', deserves special attention. There are many buildings or areas of natural beauty around the world that enjoy protected status, meaning that they benefit from central government funding and constant maintenance. C.H.M. will probably never achieve this, as it is merely a private entity and perhaps less famous now than it used to be? Perhaps this site needs the kind of support that some UK heritage sites have, from the likes of English Heritage and The National Trust? In the UK, special places of interest are supported by thousands of members paying an annual subscription or an entry fee. This secures a constant stream of funding, coupled with the fact that members often volunteer their free time to carry out much needed maintenance. I wouldn't mind betting, that it would be very easy to set up a 'friends of C.H.M.' organisation for example, where members pay an annual fee and in return, receive some small perks on-site. I would also dare to go a step further and say these proud members would also be more than happy to carry out some completely free maintenance where it was needed, for example: mark out some pitches, repair fences or clear away brambles. If this kind of 'club' existed, I would be the first to join, be keen to help and wear the t-shirt with pride, assuming there was one?

Back in 1994, I stumbled across Centre Helio Marine, completely by accident because of an advert on the back cover of a French camping and caravan guide. Today, to my knowledge, the only way a person would learn of the site would be by recommendation or a deliberate search online for a naturist resort. Even then, as some companies spend more on advertising; this is likely not to produce C.H.M. as a result. I'm sure advertising this resort is not an easy task, but if word of mouth is enough to make up the numbers, perhaps there is no need for it? I've always wished there was at least a C.H.M. t- shirt available, to proudly wear but after searching online and phoning the site, this seems not to be the case. Back in the hay day of the naturism movement in the 30's, 40's and 50's, there were many publications available, highlighting the health benefits of nudity. There were even public seminars on the subject, as organisations reached out to prospective new members. Some months ago, I was lucky enough to have visited Rome for the first time. I spent four days walking around the historic sights covering around 45 miles, this included three separate walking tours and many, many photos. The history, art, architecture, the Popes, and the influential Roman leaders captured my attention like no city ever had. If I had free time and the opportunity, I would have really enjoyed giving a talk all about my experiences and the amazing things I had learned. To be honest, I feel the same about naturism but more so, the naturism experienced in that special place in France. As far as I'm concerned, there really should be documentaries or seminars on the subject, especially in the UK for all the reasons I've already stated.

My aim has been to tell the story of the many experiences I have had, as unusual as they are. While cathartic for myself, I've also intended to entertain and perhaps educate along the way. This is not an attempt to convert the masses, as I'm fully aware that the general public think that anyone who enjoys spending time in the nude, is at best seen as a little unusual. Perhaps even in the hay day, naturists were seen as, an odd bunch that chose to ignore the norms of society and just do their own thing. The trouble for me is, that naturism and especially C.H.M. is like Rome, I've been there and seen how amazing it really is! To make things worse, as I've got older, I'm becoming more and more of a dreamer, and often find myself imagining just being there. There are occasions when I attempt to recall each of the senses and recreate the experiences in my mind. These are varied and different for each part of the site, but go something like this. If I close my eyes and imagine the smell, it is overwhelmingly the pine throughout the site which fades as you get closer to the beach. The sense of touch begins with soft pine needles on bare feet, stony paths that cause pain without sandals and then the hot but soft sand. The sensations felt on bare skin are too numerous to mention but each one sends tingles right through your body: the heat of the sun, the water, the breeze, they are all different. The sound is the sea, the wind in the trees, the entertainment at night, the waves, the laughing and chatting on the beach, the clatter of cycles, and the hub-hub of the showers, all these noises never stop in my mind. The sights are like photographs forever stored as memories, but with eyes closed as I imagine walking around the site I'm right there: the reception, the roads and tracks throughout the site, the shops and restaurants, the sports fields, the pools, the beach observation tower, the large expanse of naked people on the beach and then the evening gatherings followed by dusk. The taste is of ham and cheese in bread, water to quench my thirst, sea water in my mouth and in the evening, a large cool beer. I even have songs that remind me and take me back to my special place, these are many and forever changing but always include, 'Here comes the sun' by the Beatles and 'More than a feeling' by Boston. When I'm not dreaming in la la land, my other pastime is to check out 'You Tube', to see all the latest uploads, either featuring Montalivet coast, or C.H.M. itself. It would be unsurprising to say that I believe I have seen all of them, but as I've already suggested, a video or photo is not the same as the actual experience. Dreams and memories are what I cling to throughout the winter, whilst at the same time, I'm mentally counting down the months and the seasons in secret, until that uniquely special time comes around again.

Maybe I Will?

Hundreds of thousands of people every year bare all to the summer sun right across Europe, but society labels this practice as unusual or even something reserved for the eccentric. Does this mean that naturists have no care for what anyone thinks and have no respect for any disapproving family or friends? Is this pastime is only reserved for the amoral- adventurous-thrill-seeker, or is there another explanation? The fact that there are so many people enjoying themselves in the sun with smiles on their faces, suggests that naturists may have found something that the rest of society haven't. There are people who choose to dress up against the cold, wind, and rain just to get a little exercise, so why should doing the opposite seem weird? If money was no option, who of us wouldn't have their very own sauna and swimming pool, or constant holidays in the sun. Given the choice, we all like the nice things in life, home comforts, a nice car to drive or warm weather. When it comes down to it, naturists are no different, they are merely seeking their own enjoyable experiences but it's just that they take it to the next level.

For me naturism is very much a seasonal thing.

Apart from my constant reminiscing, the chill of the autumn and winter months mean that thoughts of getting naked couldn't be further from my mind. I find no joy in strutting around the house or laying in front of an open fire naked, it's just not my thing. However, when the winter months are gone and spring flowers burst open, there is an awakening within. As I come out of hibernation and feel the warmth of the sun on my skin, I begin to remember the pine trees and the beauty of the beach. I often wonder to myself, if there are others who feel the same way about this subject? Admittedly, the experience doesn't appeal to everyone, but as far as I'm concerned, it's only because they haven't tried it yet. However, for the final chapter, let's assume that maybe you will give it a try, but before deciding, there are some things to consider. Will you try this alone, or will you experience this with a partner? Maybe it will be with an adventurous friend, and when I say this, remember you may need to explain that true naturism is in no way sexual, it's just great fun! The decision on whether to give this a go is not easy for everyone, it may take some time to consider, not to mention a number of internal or external influences that need to be overcome. Assuming you've eventually given this a green light, the only thing left to do is decide where to go.

Once you carry out some research into the type

of venues or experiences available, you'll soon find that you're spoilt for choice. This can be an online search for UK swims, clubs or naturist beaches or you may want to search around the subject in order to have some specific questions answered. You can contact British Naturism directly online or even phone to have a chat and ask where the best place may be to start. There is also 'H&E' magazine (also available online) that has lots of information, that's if you can deal with the embarrassment of grabbing it from the top shelf of your local news agent. You may equally find many helpful online resources for European naturism, like the 'International naturist federation' or 'france4 naturism' website. If you go for a local club or 'swim' then I'd have to say that for a beginner, this is being pretty adventurous straight away. However, you could expect a warm reception from either of these, and quickly discover how friendly naturists are. While it may suit some to get stuck in and become part of a new crowd, others may choose to be less conspicuous. If its anonymity you're after, then you may first choose a quiet corner of your garden, if you have one. If this doesn't work, with some imagination and maybe a little bravery you may find a secluded beach or quiet wooded area, just to enjoy the feeling of it. Although surprisingly, you can equally feel quite anonymous without fear of being approached, attending a naturist beach or even a large naturist swim event. When one of thousands, I always felt totally anonymous in C.H.M., it was a place to totally escape, to enjoy the peace and tranquillity while at the same time loving the experience. Once you've decided where to go, it is always worth a telephone call to check admission criteria, as previously suggested some events can be a little exclusive. Quite often you will be allowed to come for an initial visit as a 'taster', but there are some who won't even allow you through the door unless you are a 'British Naturism' member. There are a range of clubs and swims, each with different requirements, some restrictive and others let anyone in. Once you're in, the trick is to relax, go with the flow and just enjoy yourself, and if it's your first time you'll be surprised how quickly you get over the nakedness and how quickly you make new friends. If you find yourself enjoying any of these venues in the UK, when you venture abroad, you'll probably be drawn to the naturist beaches and if you're lucky, real sun! Personally, I think an indoor pool in the UK compared with a French beach or a walk through a warm pine forest is no contest and so would recommend seeking a European resort, at least once a year if you get the chance.

The choice of naturist venues across France and the rest of Europe are many but there are few that stand out for their history, reputation and overall atmosphere. Albert and Christine Lecoq were pioneers back in their day, who created one of the most unique and famous naturists resorts in the world. Compared to what was on offer in the UK, I could have easily settled for one of a dozen other beaches and resorts across France but as far as I'm concerned, I happened to have stumbled upon the best. There's no escaping the fact that my own choice of naked paradise will always be C.H.M. Montalivet and for a European experience, would never recommend anywhere else. Although my personal choice will never change, there are a large selection of excellent sites across Europe and have met many naturists over the years that have their own favourites. When you're starting out on a new journey it's not the worst idea to follow a recommendation, so here's mine, for your C.H.M. visit, assuming this is your choice. Firstly, you have to consider the admission rules, as in some instances you just won't get in. The criteria have changed over the years and back in 1994 it was quite different than it is today. Holding an I.N.F. membership card was mandatory back then, but you were able to purchase one as you entered the resort. In 2003 we had to purchase this before we entered, even though we came as a couple, but luckily a British Naturism card also included International Naturist Federation membership, so obtaining this was easy. Today if you want to enter

C.H.M, an I.N.F. membership is not compulsory and in fact, even if you are a member, this won't necessarily get you inside the gates. Providing there are spaces, if you turn up as a couple, and that's any couple combination with identification, you get in. If you want to go to C.H.M. as a group, that's no problem at all; this could be a large extended family but also could mean a group of friends, male, female or mixed. Although if this is a particularly large group, there may be additional criteria applied. If you try to get in as a single person, male or female, you will be denied, unless you are a regular visitor. However, if you are introduced by a regular visitor, which means someone who has been many times or at least once a year, you will be allowed in. These rules apply whether you are staying on site or come in as a day visitor. You are also permitted entry as a day visitor if you are staying at another naturist resort, as they can act as an introducer in the same way. These rules apply for summers leading up to 2020 but to avoid disappointment, a phone call before turning up is recommended. For most of the year, booking ahead for a camping pitch or touring caravan is not an absolute necessity, but over the summer holiday season from July 10th to 30th August, it is a must. On my sixth visit in early August, I discovered to my detriment how necessary it was to book a pitch. After travelling all the way from England, I had to turn around and leave reception through the same door I entered, head hung low, with nowhere to stay. Luckily, I was able to spend the first two nights at the municipal campsite on the opposite side of la avenue de Europe. Although down hearted, this was no big problem as I was able to enter as a day visitor which allows entry right up to midnight. If you are planning a tent as accommodation then you have a choice, large tent pitch, small tent, electric or not. If you don't ask for a small pitch with no electrics, you may pay a little more than you need to. Although I love the experience of camping, occasionally I do feel slightly envious of those in superior surroundings. In order that nothing adversely influences your first experience, if you get the chance, I recommend you go posh and sample some of the wide range of mobile homes, wooden houses or glamping tents available.

In many ways over the years, I have found the travel to a holiday destination can really add to the whole experience. If it's simplicity you want, with limited hassle, fly to Bordeaux and hire a car, or if expense is no option, go by taxi. There are a surprising number of Brits who drive down to Bordeaux, often with caravan in tow, then turn north and follow the coast up to Montalivet. It is worth a note at this point that if you are following an interactive map from Bordeaux, this will bypass Montalivet town and bring you towards the site, cross country through the forests. Although this is more direct, it is far less fun as you miss the many road signs for Centre Helio Marin along the way and in the town itself. As you pass Montilavet town hall you get to see a slice of history, as this was the building where the first lease was signed for the resort back in July 1950. If you fancy a bit of romance and are not concerned how long it takes, you could always take a first-class ticket aboard the overnight sleeper train from Paris to Bordeaux, a trip I would love to take again in the future, even only for memories sake. Whatever mode of travel you choose, after some hours you'll arrive at the front gates, and reception of Centre Helio Marin, La Avenue de Europe, Montalivet. If you have come by car, caravan or mobile home, do not drive up to the entry gates as you may to be asked to reverse away, instead try to find a parking spot that's not causing too much congestion and head for reception by foot. In the summer months, reception can be busy, but eventually a helpful member of staff will deal with your admission and answer all your questions. The reception service is so good, that they will even offer to show you to your pitch if required.

If you've never been to a large naturist resort, the first few minutes can feel a little surreal. Perhaps the first thing to do, is concentrate on setting up camp or finding your pitch. The actual disrobing part can happen whenever you want it to and whenever you're comfortable. My advice is to head straight for the beach or if the weather is restrictive, one of the pools or health suite. You can almost guarantee that's it not what you expected, and it will be far more exciting than you ever imagined. Any nervousness you experience by being naked for the first time, will dissipate in minutes. Instead of feeling vulnerable, after a short time there is an undoubtable feeling of freedom from the hang ups you once had. As I found back in 1994, you instantly become one of the multitudes and blend in. In fact, you'll quickly find that you're more worried about applying sun block than the fact that you're naked.

By the time you make it to the beach, you'll have already sampled the atmosphere and understand that C.H.M. is very much a resort for all generations. In this relaxed untainted atmosphere, you'll soon discover that all your cares and worries melt away, as both literally and metaphorically, everything is stripped away. The chaos of life seems a thing of the past, as you sit and ponder things in a new way. Instead of obeying the clock and routines, you'll only leave the beach if you are hungry or if the clouds obscure the sun. If you've travelled to Monatlivet and made it to this special beach, there is only one thing left to do....... soak up the atmosphere and with a smile on your face enjoy this new experience. You have now become one of the lucky few who have visited not only the first official naturist beach in France but perhaps the most iconic nudist resort in the world!

The end.